POWER PODCASTING

How to Start a Podcast That Grows Your Sphere of Influence

Derek L. Zboran
www.ProfessionalPodcastCreation.com

NMMP™
New Media Marketing Pro Books
www.NewMediaMarketingPro.com

Power Podcasting: How to Start a Podcast That Grows Your Sphere of Influence

Derek L. Zboran

ISBN-10: 0-9844331-0-4

ISBN-13: 978-0-9844331-0-0

Published by New Media Marketing Pro Books, an imprint of the Jim Zboran Group.

Derek L. Zboran, Podcaster

New Media Marketing Pro Books

PO BOX 1860

Rolla, MO 65401

www.ProfessionalPodcastCreation.com

www.NewMediaMarketingPro.com

Derek Zboran is available to be interviewed on your podcast or to help coach you in developing a podcast that builds your professional network.

Email derek@professionalpodcastcreation.com for more information.

Written by a growing professional in new media and marketing.

Derek L. Zboran is an author, podcast host, course creator, and a growing expert in the fields of new media, communication, and professional development. He has helped over five hundred college students get better grades in school with his online courses about how to study and learn. Through his podcasting work, he has had the opportunity to interview over fifty world-class individuals, including best-selling authors, musicians, and award-winning business owners.

Derek L. Zboran has forged connections with a variety of creative professionals by adopting the role of an interviewer. In this book, he reveals how you can use similar strategies to build your sphere of influence in a community that matters to you. Everything is explained step by step. When you are finished with this book, you will be ready to launch a podcast that grows your sphere of influence and creates value-based connections with important people in your niche.

Do you want to work one-on-one with Derek Zboran to help you develop your podcast? He is working with creatives in a variety of niches. Email him at derek@professionalpodcastcreation.com or visit www.ProfessionalPodcastCreation.com.

This book contains everything you need to know to launch a successful podcast.

To help increase your chances of success, I am making a special resource available to those who have purchased this book.

Get my free PDF *Interview Like a Pro: 5 Types of Questions that Spark Powerful Podcast Conversations* for free at the link below to help you put the ideas in this book to use!

You can get it at this link:

www.ProfessionalPodcastCreation.com/powerpodcastingbonus.com

Table of Contents

WORKING WITH DEREK:

Foreword by Rebecca Buckley

Derek Zboran has worked at the Rolla Public Library for over two years, and I have had the pleasure of being library director during this time. Derek's initiative, creativity, and professionalism have furthered the reach of our library program in a huge way.

He came along at the perfect time during the COVID spread to lead us in our first virtual programming with patrons of all ages. Derek quickly learned and then taught some of our staff video editing for our regular weekly Story Times, activity programs, and more. We held two very popular and vibrant online Summer Reading Programs during the COVID summers of 2020 and 2021. The first year's programming was entirely online, and the second year's was a hybrid of online and in-person.

After our first successful summer program, Derek expanded his video skills and began periodically interviewing members of our community. He connected our library brand to local business brands such as Soda & Scoops, Kristina's Casa, and Town & Country Bank by filming collaborative programs for kids that we aired on our social media pages. These programs featured business profiles, interviews, and a story—all at an interest level appropriate for young people.

The 2021 summer program was a bicentennial year for Missouri, and Derek filmed a regular Missouri Bicentennial Series that summer that initiated positive connections between the library and significant academic leaders all across Missouri, such as John McManus, Diana Ahmad, Steven Watts, Chuck Haddix, and Gary Kremer. He filmed four interview projects with our local Phelps County Historical Society that gained thousands of views on social media and generated positive buzz about both the library and the historical society. Underpinning these interviews were quality questions in which Derek did his research and came prepared for thoughtful conversations.

Derek is a team player who is excited by challenges and loves a project! He has been an immense asset to the library and has helped our brand grow positively across the Midwest. I have been so proud to have him on staff, and his collaborative work within our community has been outreach that has extended the library's mission in such a relevant and modern way in our community. Derek's interviewing skills (via video or audio) have been a perfect way to connect to our neighbors in Rolla.

These library/community programs Derek has led have been impactful beyond just a week or so of views on social media. Those partners have reached out to us again and again, sometimes even with donation funds for our library programs!

Connection is always a major aim in Derek's personal and professional pursuits, and he has succeeded in helping us create a growing community network through his high quality and ever-adapting programming work over the past two years at the Rolla Public Library. We are all the better for it!

If you are like Derek and recognize that creating value-based connections is important to expanding your influence in any community, I encourage you to read and enjoy this book!

Rebecca Buckley, MLIS

Director of the Rolla Public Library

CHAPTER ONE:

Are You Ready to Start Talking To World-Class Professionals in Your Niche?

"At what point are you ready to talk to world-class professionals?"

This is the question that surfaces in my brain moments before my interview with A. J. Baime. He's a New York Times best-selling author. I'm a skinny kid from Missouri working in a public library. Our conversation was part of a video podcast series I was doing on behalf of the Rolla Public Library. It featured interviews with top historians and authors. Our potential audience included thousands of patrons who follow the library's profiles on Facebook and YouTube. My eyes locked into the dark eye of the webcam like those of a deer who is just about to get obliterated by a semitruck. I smile. It's LIVE. I anxiously stutter and stumble over an introduction I improvise on the spot. Then my guest takes over the conversation.

Baime thanks me and the library for inviting him to discuss his research, expertise, and unique insights. Last year he had written a book about the 1948 presidential election titled *Dewey Defeats Truman*. It was about Harry S. Truman's decision to run for president against the expectations of powerful political enemies, educated critics, and bewildered advisors. Baime revealed personal details about how he discovered and interacted with Truman's legacy. He takes a moment to show a portrait of the 33rd president, which had hung in his dad's office. Suddenly, I hit the wrong button, and my guest disappeared from the livestream. Whoops! Within a few split seconds, I got him back on. "Sorry about that, A. J.," I yelp. My guest shrugs it off and doesn't miss a beat. We begin a back-and-forth conversation about the content of the book.

My guest is a journalist who writes regularly for *The Wall Street Journal.* Therefore, it is no surprise that he synthesizes the answers to my questions in engaging and colorful ways. Things go well. And about twenty minutes into the interview, I notice something changing inside me. I feel myself thinking less about me. And instead, I'm focusing more on his answers and our conversation. The knots in my stomach loosen. Breathing becomes easier. At one point, I ask a question that makes my guest pause. Any newbie interviewer will tell you that silence can induce crippling anxiety. "Wonderful question," he says before launching into an answer. By the end of the interview, my anxiety had morphed into confidence. Afterwards, we chatted for a few minutes off the record. "Your questions were great; keep in touch," he said enthusiastically. He even offered to buy me a beer the next time he visited Missouri.

I began that interview scared, insecure, uncertain. But I left with confidence that I could talk to any successful person in the world if I engaged them in the right type of conversation and in an effective "space." With this confidence came an important realization. Networking with world-class professionals is easier than most people think. In fact, by starting a podcast, a variety of professionals can create a powerful space for connection in a world that increasingly values diverse perspectives, thoughtfully engaged community members, and authentic conversations.

There's no doubt you recognize the importance of networking. A LinkedIn survey found that 80 percent of professionals understand that building connections with other people is crucial to their professional success. The question isn't whether or not you should network. Instead, we must ask, how do we engage others in authentic and meaningful ways?

I have discovered that launching an interview podcast can provide twenty-first-century professionals with amazing opportunities to make a bigger impact and connect with more people who are significant in one's niche. Launching the right kind of podcast will empower you to immediately begin establishing value-based connections with world-class professionals in your niche, industry, or career field.

CEO, entrepreneur, and best-selling author Keith Ferrazzi wrote that "Poverty... wasn't only a lack of financial resources; it was isolation from the kind of people who could help you make more of yourself." Look at your current professional network. Do you ever feel isolated, lonely, or disconnected from your industry or niche? You are experiencing a form of poverty. It leaves your professional goals and ambitions malnourished. The remedy is establishing connections one person at a time by creating and exchanging value.

Could you benefit from connecting with other people in your area of interest? People you want to connect with have busy and stressful lives. They have priorities they are struggling to manage. They also have shorter attention spans than ever before. Making really valuable connections in this environment remains crucial even if it is more difficult than ever before. By far, asking someone to connect for an interview, where you ask thoughtful questions, is an amazing way to forge connections. And you're doing it the right way because you are providing value. (Yes, interviews provide your contacts with value. You'll learn more about that in chapter four.)

Ferrazzi suggests a multitude of ways to connect with other people in his classic book about networking, titled *Never Eat Alone.* All of them are oriented around a simple but powerful idea: that the "Great myth of networking is that you start reaching out to others only when you need something," but that the reality is "People who have the largest circle of contacts, mentors, and friends know that you must reach out to others long before you need anything at all... [you are] constantly creating the environment and community you want for yourself, no matter what may occur." His book is about how to cultivate your community before you need it. Podcasting is not one of the ideas he shares. But it should be on your radar because it is a powerful way to build a community of influence.

You can rapidly grow your sphere of influence at any stage of your career when you launch a podcast that fosters authentic conversations with significant people in your field. Desire a job in a certain industry? Start a podcast in which you interview professionals in that field. Wish you could gain traction in a particular niche? Interview the people who form the community behind that niche. Are you a traditional brick-and-mortar business owner who wants to become more engaged in your community? Start a podcast that allows you to connect with peers, customers, and community leaders.

Professionals at all levels are using the podcast space as an opportunity to interview a variety of successful people. In so doing, they are building connections that expand confidence, opportunity, and even knowledge about current happenings in their field of expertise. This is a strategy that works well if you're a young person and still building a reputation in your niche or industry. It also works well if you are an experienced person who has not yet prioritized professional networking. Launching an interview podcast creates YOUR space for interacting with top thinkers, doers, and achievers.

Who can utilize this podcast strategy? The answer is anybody who wants to actively engage in a particular niche, industry, or career in a meaningful and community-oriented way. That means;

- Business owners
- Entrepreneurs
- Community leaders
- Health and wellness experts
- Activists
- Scholars
- Writers

- Thought leaders
- Religious figures
- Public servants
- Journalists

All careers, projects, institutions, and movements depend on people and communities. Therefore, there is a wide range of professionals who can use the podcast strategies discussed in this book.

When you first start a podcast, many coaches and how-to guides will recommend that you start listening to popular interview-based programs. Which ones do they recommend? NPR's *Fresh Air* and *The Joe Rogan Experience* are routinely cited as podcasts that are valuable for aspiring podcasters to devour, understand, and perhaps even emulate. I agree that you can learn from listening to these shows. And it is a good idea for people who enter the podcast sphere to be familiar with what is working in the world of audio storytelling. But you must also remember that both shows are produced with big budgets. Millions of people listen to these podcasts every week. If you are starting out and you want to use podcasting to build your sphere of influence, do not try to be the next Terry Gross or Joe Rogan.

Instead, put your focus on creating a space for authentic conversations with people who matter in your niche or industry. Your goal should not be to become a media personality. It should be to create a space for authentic conversations that are perceived as valuable by your audience and the people you interview. Exchanging value through authentic conversations is the ticket to growing your sphere of influence using the podcast strategies discussed in this book.

Networking doesn't begin when you are ready. You become ready by taking action today in ways that are authentic, ethical, and effective. Think back to the things you succeeded with in your life. Did you feel ready before you took action and got results? Many of us feel like we will never be ready to undertake a massive project like a weekly podcast. We don't think we're qualified. But the truth is that you are 100 percent ready to take action if you are willing to position yourself in a way that is authentic.

Many scoff when I tell them that they can host a podcast and start booking amazing guests right away. But I've done it in three different podcast-style projects. And I'm not the only one who is landing top-notch guests. Consider the story of a podcaster named Jaime Masters (formerly Jaime Tardy.) She's a business coach. Her podcast is called *The Eventual Millionaire.* Each week she interviews an exceptionally wealthy person. Jaime's podcast reveals the stories, perspectives, and insights of the financially successful.

She must be a millionaire with instant access to lots of rich people, right? Wrong. Despite the fact that each week she lands top guests on her show, she herself is not a millionaire. "I don't have a million-dollar net worth yet," she wrote on her podcast's website. So what entitles her to talk to these people? Positioning is the key. "The reason why I've interviewed over 350 multimillionaire entrepreneurs… [is] I'm searching for the experiences, stories, and resources these leaders have used to make millionaire money… Each week I bring to you a new millionaire to learn from, providing you with their best tactics, resources, and advice for growing your business." Jaime created an authentic space to interview these people for her show, and the space works as a mechanism for connection.

Jaime is a business coach, and she can ask questions that are interesting, thoughtful, and relevant. By positioning herself as an "eventual millionaire," she accomplishes two things. First, she is attracting other people who have set ambitious financial goals. This is her audience. These are people who will listen to her show, appreciate what she is doing, and become fans. Second, she leverages her curiosity and her current accomplishments to create a valuable space for authentic conversations.

Creating a space where you can be authentically YOU is one of the most critical parts of the podcast strategies described in this book. Imagine if Jaime claimed that she was extraordinarily wealthy? Or an expert on how to be a millionaire? She would come off as inauthentic, and her podcast space wouldn't work for networking. When you try to be inauthentic, you rob yourself of meaningful connections. Authenticity matters more than anything when you are doing a podcast. It helps you recruit guests with confidence. It helps you engage in deep conversations with those who agree to be interviewed. People who will form the basis of your audience will love you and what you're doing. And it sets the right stage for future interactions with any person you interview.

You may be wondering if the ideas I write about in this book can help you expand your sphere of influence and increase your opportunities. Of course they can! My own experience illustrates just how effectively podcasts can help you win friends and influence people in the age of podcasting.

Over the last two to three years, I've conducted forty-plus interviews and have led three podcast-style projects. I've talked to some of the world's top talent in fields relevant to my interests and current work. I've talked to best-selling authors such as A. J. Baime from California and respected professors of history here in Missouri such as Diana Ahmad, Steven Watts, and John C. McManus. I've done two interviews with radio DJ Chuck Haddix, who has spent decades hosting a show that currently airs on NPR's flagship station KCUR-FM 89.3 in Kansas City. I've chatted with Postmodern Jukebox musicians who have appeared in viral YouTube videos. And I've talked to significant business owners and professionals located in the vicinity where I live and work.

As a young man who is growing into a successful career as a communications professional, each of these interviews created valuable connections with other professional people. By conducting these interviews, I have also enhanced my brand by demonstrating how I am an engaged member of the community who is curious, eager to learn, and willing to hear a diverse range of perspectives regarding topics that relate to my passion in fields such as history, music, and self-improvement.

The idea of good networking is to build your connections before you need them. Podcasting helps you initiate contacts and exchange value with them by giving you the space to conduct thoughtful interviews. Possibilities for what can be done through podcasting are just beginning to be explored. According to data collected by Edison Research and reported in *NPR's Podcast Start*

Up Guide, podcast consumption in the United States alone expanded in almost every consecutive year between 2007 and 2019. It's estimated that there were over two million podcasts in 2021. For every major podcast host such as Joe Rogan and Terry Gross, you'll find literally thousands of indie podcasters. Some are aspiring radio hosts. Some are kids having fun talking about topics they love. But many of them are professionals in a given niche or industry. And they're using podcasts to create spaces in which they can connect with significant people in their community and exchange value through meaningful conversations.

Podcasting is a powerful tool that twenty-first-century professionals are using to grow and strengthen their professional networks. Initiating contacts and establishing a basic level of rapport with them can be frustratingly difficult in an age of so many distractions, stress, and overwhelm. Hosting a decent interview-based podcast literally gives you the space to talk to the rock stars of your niche or industry for fifteen, thirty, or even sixty minutes. Imagine yourself six months from now, hosting your own podcast, conversing with world-class professionals. You're curious. They share their expertise, experiences, and knowledge. They feel valued and thank YOU for the opportunity to share themselves in a space where they are valued. As you build rapport with person after person in your niche, you morph from poverty in your personal network to a powerful sphere of personal influence that is ethical, authentic, and based on real value exchange. Connections you have as a podcast host can have relevance to your professional network far beyond your podcast.

Regardless of whether you're a beginning professional or an experienced one, you can rapidly grow your sphere of influence at any stage of your career by launching a podcast that fosters authentic conversations with significant people in your niche or industry. By embracing podcasts and stepping into the role of the interviewer, you can connect with scores of world-class professionals and remedy an impoverished professional network. Let's get started on this journey to becoming a better-connected professional with more opportunity and confidence!

CHAPTER TWO:

Networking Can Be Hard but Launching a Podcast Can Put You into the Center of Your Niche

My finger hovered anxiously over the big blue button. I reread the brief and polite message I had crafted requesting a connection. "Don't kid yourself," one of the negative voices in my head declared. "He's not going to respond to some unknown kid." Turns out those little voices are sometimes correct. My request for connection was ignored.

Just before entering the workforce, I had created a LinkedIn profile. It was a big deal for me. I had worked on some small online MOOCs (Massive Open Online Courses) offered by Coursera and edX. But aside from that, I had not really engaged in social media activity. It was exciting to start thinking about setting goals as an adult, thinking about my personal brand, and considering how I might begin cultivating relationships with other professionals.

I immediately began thinking about people I might add as connections. I thought of a YouTuber who was highly inspirational to me at the time. He did a podcast about succeeding in college and personal development. At the time, I also had a website on how to excel in college. So I looked him up, and his LinkedIn profile came right up in the search results. I carefully typed out a brief message asking for his connection. Then I smashed the connect button. Weeks passed, and I never heard back. Of course, I didn't take it personally. He probably never even saw the request. But it is discouraging when your efforts to connect with other professionals fail.

Keith Ferrazzi wrote in his book *Never Eat Alone* that, "We are the very product of the people and networks to which we are connected. Who you know determines who you are—how you feel, how you act, and what you achieve." And as mentioned in the previous chapter, he also accurately described poverty as ". . . isolation from the kind of people who could help you make more of yourself."

For many professionals, it is a challenge to improve and expand our networks. New professionals such as myself are still building successes. We're often not sure of how best to get our foot in the door. Unless you come from a well-connected family, young people have a lot of work to do in terms of building connections between themselves and the outside world.

And what about older professionals? Many struggle to change careers later in life. And many love their career or industry of choice but have not yet prioritized networking and recognize that they need more quality connections to increase their opportunities.

Most people know that they need to reach out and engage the people in their niche, industry, or career. And if you are holding this book, it means you think podcasting can give you opportunities to engage your network and grow your sphere of influence.

Just knowing a podcast can help you expand your professional network does not mean it is easy to launch one. One challenge that emerges for many is thinking about where to begin. There are dozens of well-written books about how to start a podcast. The internet is filled with gurus who are all clamoring to tell you everything you need to do to start an amazing interview program. It can be difficult to navigate through all the ideas, research, and tips to find just exactly what you need to do to create a podcast space that allows you to connect with others in meaningful ways.

Much of the how-to content on podcasting is about how to earn bundles of profits from your podcast or how to build successful media companies. They are not written specifically for professionals who want to leverage podcasting to create a professional networking space. When you create a podcast specifically to grow your sphere of influence by leveraging the power of the interview, you need to be able to make the right moves and avoid all the rabbit holes that suck away your time, attention, and money.

What often stops people from creating powerful podcasts that help them expand their spheres of influence? Common issues include:

- **They fear the role of the interviewer.** Isn't that for journalists like Lester Holt or Maria Bartiromo? Or for personalities like Bill Maher or Greg Gutfeld? Actually, no! Chances are good that you play the role of interviewer every day. Asking questions is a natural and effective way for us to connect with our fellow humans. You ask your friends and family questions. You ask your colleagues and peers questions. When you have difficulty leveraging the role of the interviewer, you miss opportunities to connect with top thinkers, doers, and achievers in your niche through your podcast.

- **They don't have a clear internal sense of what inspires them about their niche.** You must define this. Every conversation has a "why." There is intention behind all questions and conversations. Good podcasts are hosted by people who understand their why at a deep, personal, and engaging level. They conduct interviews in a way that reflects that intention naturally and engagingly. Understanding your why helps you create an effective space for conducting podcast interviews.

- **They don't know how to organize their efforts and recordings into a polished podcast show.** Isn't that really hard and expensive? The answer is no, if you do it the right way, and don't get sucked down rabbit holes that devour your time and money.

- **They fear the idea of recruiting guests.** A lot of would-be podcasters are mortified by the idea of inviting guests on a show to interview them for thirty, forty-five, or sixty minutes. The idea of interviewing anybody, and especially successful people we may only barely know, is a stressor.

- **They don't know how to prepare for an interview.** If you do it right, a natural conversation happens. Many people sound too rigid because they overprepare and are unwilling to let the conversation take on a life of its own. Or they underprepare and simply ask the guest to rehash lots of stuff everybody already knows. Not only does this make for a boring interview to listen to, it does not establish the kind of connection you want to create through your podcast interviews.

- **Technology becomes a problem.** Should you get the Shure SM7B or the Audio-Technica ATR2100 when you go shopping for your microphone? What does a pop filter do? Is Zoom good enough to record a podcast interview, or do you need some other type of virtual studio? What happens when you stop recording? Answers to these questions can lead people all over the place. Many either don't take action because they are overwhelmed, or they waste resources by investing time, energy, and money in "solutions" that aren't right for the kind of podcast they want to make.

- **The idea of talking to people scares a lot of would-be podcast hosts.** "What if my guest doesn't like me? What if they think my questions are stupid?" Fear of rejection can even cause people to neglect taking action on their podcast.

Take a step back from podcasting and consider how you want to be remembered. What things will you have achieved? What experiences will you have had? What legacy will you leave behind? You need to initiate, nurture, and satisfy relationships with other people to make your professional goals happen. Even those of us who consider ourselves individualists must engage with other people and make a difference in the communities in which we interact. Podcasting can help you, but you must take the right actions. Your relevance is at stake.

It is not easy to take action on a podcast that can radically expand your professional network and enhance your personal brand.

In 2021, I knew I wanted to start a full-blown audio podcast that would become available on sites like Spotify and Stitcher. But for at least two months, I waited to take action. I was fearful about reaching out to people who I considered outside my social orbit or who I thought would be uninterested in talking to me.

I did not even begin to understand the true power of podcasts for professionals. I was infatuated with the idea of podcasting as a rebellious new form of media. But I lacked a serious understanding of how it could be used to empower professionals and the communities they serve.

Originally, I was nervous about playing the role of interviewer. Sometimes I stutter. Often I stumble over words. Wouldn't I embarrass myself?

I lacked the kind of road map that I needed to build a podcast that was right for my goals and limited resources. Most of the books and articles I read on the topic were about how to build shows like those hosted by superstars such as Terry Gross or Joe Rogan. It has never been my intention to be a media personality. (Not to mention I don't have access to big budgets and large teams.)

I took the best steps I could. And I made my way through a wilderness of confusion. I learned how to set the right priorities when it came to podcasting—to leverage its power in an authentic way that really brought value to myself and others. I learned how to accept my voice and to work on ways to improve it. And I developed a road map that can help me advance my professional pursuits in a meaningful, exciting, and fun way that truly feels "connected" to communities I care about.

You already know that enhancing your personal brand, serving a community you're passionate about, and growing your sphere of influence requires work. Podcasting, like any other networking strategy, will mean an investment of effort.

Expanding your sphere of influence through podcasting is difficult. As Kristen Meinzer reports in her book, *So You Want to Start a Podcast*, as few as "16 percent of podcasts have published more than nine episodes." In other words, most podcasts go belly-up before they reach the tenth episode. Being recognized for creating a valuable space, for sharing valuable insights, and for offering compelling conversations in a market crowded with too many podcasts does not come without working hard and taking the right steps. If you have tried to create a podcast and have failed in the past, or if you have tried other networking strategies that have been unsuccessful, it is important that you realize the problem is not with you. It is with how you are applying yourself to your specific networking challenges.

In a world of millions of podcasts, MOST do fail. But you have what it takes to achieve great results. Approach the ideas you read about here in this book with an open mind. Apply them. Take consistent action, and you will notice that with each step, you increasingly feel the confidence, credibility, and authority that comes from hosting a podcast that allows you to connect in meaningful conversations with the people in your niche and industry. Taking this journey will transform your brand and the concept of the value you provide, and it will empower the way you connect to the communities you want to impact.

Many of you might wonder if you are ready to build a professional network. Are you too young to build your sphere of influence? Do you have enough experience in your niche, industry, or career? The truth is that if you are reading this book, you are ready to get started growing your sphere of influence. What this all boils down to is having authentic and value-based connections with the people you want in your professional circle—at any stage of your career.

Many might be wondering if you can actually get great guests. "I don't think I can get great guests," was a belief I had when I first started podcasting. Action-taking and experience have taught me this was a false and limiting myth. When I started taking action, I was shocked as I pitched big-league guests, and they were more than willing to be interviewed for my podcast projects. I still get nervous when I reach out to potential interviewees. Surely not everyone you pitch to be on your podcast will accept your invitation. But many guests will be happy to be on your show when you invite them in the right way. When you follow a commonsense approach to recruiting guests, you will be shocked at how easy it is to get world-class people to appear on your show and will feel great for having done so.

Some people hesitate to start a podcast because they don't think they know enough about their niche, industry, or career. How much do you need to know? If you are trying to grow your sphere of influence in a certain field, chances are good that you care about that field. You are reading books related to the topic. You are following celebrities and leaders in the field. It's something you think about while working out at the gym, cooking dinner, or folding your laundry. You know more than you think. And frankly, for an interview podcast, you needn't know a lot anyway. Though the more you know, the better. (More on that in a coming chapter.) All you really need is curiosity and the ability to follow some simple tactics that beginning journalists use to conduct interviews that are courteous, respectful, and authentic.

Finally, a big concern among many is the idea of launching a podcast itself. "I've never done a podcast before," they tell me. "Isn't it hard and expensive?" It certainly can be! Especially when you Google search podcasting or read some of the how-to guides out there, and they go on for paragraphs about how to hire creative teams and the thousands of dollars of equipment you need to sound professional. You will not find such advice in this book. I encourage people to start with minimal setups and scale up afterwards. I will share exactly what I used to record the first ten episodes of my podcast. This does not have to be hard. You can sound great using tools you already have or those which can be purchased affordably.

The question should not be, "Am I ready?" It should be, "When should I take action?" And hopefully, you realize that you are ready to take action now, regardless of how much experience you have had with podcasts or your current professional status.

We live in a marketing era where success depends on educating others. Therefore, creating a space where we exchange value by being curious and learning from the insights, experiences, and challenges of others is a particularly advantageous networking opportunity. We engage audiences at the same time as we build our network.

Professionals in a variety of niches, industries, and careers are creating interview podcasts to stand out from the crowd, connect with significant people, and build bigger spheres of influence with interviews. The world we live in today is one that will be increasingly defined by those with a willingness to engage diverse communities, forge authentic relationships, and exchange value by having meaningful conversations. Each person has within themselves the ability to engage more proactively with significant people. And as you engage the right way, your sphere of influence will grow, expand, and prosper.

CHAPTER THREE:

What Does It Take To Launch a Successful Podcast?

Maybe you are a new professional, working to build a strong professional network largely from scratch. Or perhaps you are an experienced professional just now starting to prioritize relationships in your field of interest. Either way, you are going to benefit when you use podcasting to create a space for constructive conversations with top thinkers, doers, and achievers in your niche.

My experience in podcasting consists of over forty interviews with a wide range of professionals. I've engaged in conversations with musicians, business owners, historians, best-selling authors, and other significant doers and achievers. Conducting quality conversations expands my professional network in powerful ways. It can expand yours too!

As Keith Ferrazzi argues in *Never Eat Alone*, successful professionals initiate relationships and build networks before they are needed. Podcasting provides you with amazing opportunities to initiate those contacts and expand your network in ways that exchange value.

Also, through conducting interviews, you will increasingly gain respect for a range of worldviews. Your own perspective will become more rounded and educated as you seek to understand the perspectives of others. You will find yourself developing a healthier curiosity about your niche and the community which you seek to serve and impact. This will position you for greater success in a professional environment that increasingly depends on continuous learning and the ability to work with other professionals from a diverse range of backgrounds.

The basic steps for building your networking through podcasting are outlined in this chapter. Each of these steps will be fleshed out in future chapters. For now, this is just a bird's-eye view of what you will be working on as you read this book and apply the action steps I outline in future chapters.

Step into the role of interviewer with confidence.

Who can step into the role of the interviewer?

Maybe you think of news journalists like Lester Holt or Maria Bartiromo engaging in serious conversations with people who are making headlines. Or maybe your mind conjures up images of light discussions with icons like Johnny Carson, David Letterman, and Jay Leno. Perhaps you think of Mike Wallace engaging in deep and thoughtful conversations with all the artists, writers, and cultural figures who appeared on his show. Each of these media professionals are interviewers.

They ask questions with intention from a place of authenticity, and they do so in a space that creates the context for high-stakes conversations.

Every recorded conversation feels like a high-stakes conversation, hence the reason some have called interviews "conversations with consequences." People prepare for them. They take them seriously. Interviews sharpen instincts and focus attention. The best interviews are those in which you experience a connection through the conversation.

If you can ask intentional questions authentically and respect diverse perspectives, you can conduct interviews that grow your sphere of influence. This is the type of interviewer who confidently initiates contact with significant doers, thinkers, and achievers in his or her niche.

Your podcast provides the space for a meaningful dialogue. And through quality engagement with your guest, you will often create a connection that lasts longer than the podcast interview. This is what expands your influence and opportunities in the community you seek to serve as a professional.

Create an engaging space for conversations through your podcast.

Podcasts fail when they are based on poorly thought-through concepts.

Simple, relevant, and engaging podcast concepts succeed!

When you take time to identify crucial elements of your podcast, you create a space that will attract interesting guests, foster better conversations, and help you build a bigger sphere of influence.

What steps must one take to define their podcast space? They include;

- Considering your personal brand.
- Answering some basic questions about your potential audience and what content they are already consuming.
- Creating an avatar of your target listener.
- Crafting a basic elevator pitch that will appeal to your future audience and guests.

You, the interviewer, will make a better connection with your guest if the context in which you conduct the interview is a podcast with a solid foundation. This book will help get you started with a solid foundation that sets you up for success.

Define a flexible podcast structure.

Flexibility is one of the benefits of podcasting. But even podcasts that leverage this benefit know that defining some basic structure can be helpful.

If you create a simple and organized structure for your podcast episodes, then your show will sound more professional, episodes will be easier to produce, and you will be better equipped to wow potential guests!

Discussing your podcast's structure is about answering some of the basic questions, like "How long should my episodes be?" or "How should I begin each episode?" or "Should I include music?" These are the kind of structural questions that will help define how listeners experience your show. You want a structure that is professional and helps define the space in which you want to have conversations.

Recruit awesome guests to be interviewed for your podcast.

I've recruited all sorts of interesting guests for my podcasting projects, including a New York Times best-selling author, an award-winning jazz vocalist, and a saxophone player who has performed in Postmodern Jukebox videos that have been viewed tens of millions of times. What's the secret to getting world-class professionals on your podcast?

Be proactive. Ask fearlessly. Sure, you'll get ignored by a lot of people. But some, and perhaps many, will say yes and fully enjoy the interview experience you provide them with your questions.

Getting amazing guests for my podcast projects helps make my show more interesting. I become more passionate about the project when I initiate contact with the people who are rock stars in my field of interest.

Because interviews are how you connect with others, you can only grow your sphere of influence when you reach out to guests and pitch them effectively.

As you begin this process, you will experience moments of euphoria as amazing guests agree to appear on your podcast. You will also encounter moments of disappointment when a guest you really wanted does not reply to an email you sent.

All things considered, if you reach out to twenty or thirty potential interviewees using the best practices you will learn in this book, you will likely gain five or six interview "accepts" from outstanding guests. And this is more than enough to launch your podcast and lay the foundation for getting more success later as your podcast grows.

Prepare for successful conversations with your interviewees.

After you have reached out to several potential interviewees and some come back with "Yes," what next? How do you plan for a spontaneous conversation that has yet to happen? Should you write out all your questions ahead of time?

Some people claim they do not prepare for interviews because it makes the conversation less authentic. Personally, I have discovered that some basic preparation increases my confidence and helps me engage the interviewee at a deeper level more quickly.

You can successfully interview people for your podcast when you take simple steps to prepare for your conversation ahead of time. How much prep work? That depends on several factors, including how much time you can invest, your personal interview style, and your level of experience. Even just an hour or two of preparation before your conversation can help you ask better questions, get better answers, and create a more meaningful connection with the person you are talking with.

Set up your virtual recording studio.

How does a guy here in rural Missouri talk to world-class jazz musicians over in New York or best-selling authors in California? It is all thanks to advanced technology. Thankfully, you do not need to be a tech wizard to create your own virtual studio where you can record interviews with awesome guests from around the world.

When beginner podcasters get started, they should begin with options that involve minimal expense and minimal learning curves. There are relatively inexpensive options out there that are affordable and will help you sound great. Entire books have been written about what equipment and software one needs to launch a good podcast. For this book, I am going to recommend a setup that will work great for shoestring budgets. Some of the equipment you may already own!

Getting started simply will help you put the focus where it belongs. Your focus should be on getting great interview guests and making meaningful connections with them. As your success with podcasting grows, you can always scale up your setup and make yourself sound even more professional.

Click the Record button and interview a world-class person.

You've reached out to awesome people and invited them to be interviewed on your podcast. You have scheduled times to talk. Now comes the big day when you first do an interview!

The best way to learn how to do interviews is to do them over and over and to continuously improve your skills and confidence. There are also some simple interviewing best practices that, if followed, will help you get great results immediately and provide a foundation for you to further develop your skills.

When you accept your interview abilities as they are today, and proactively work to improve your conversation skills by focusing on areas for improvement, you will make stronger connections with your guests, have more engaging conversations, and grow your sphere of influence.

Grow in confidence as an interviewer.

There is always a bit of self-doubt that happens before and even after an interview concludes. If you apply some of the basic best practices you will learn from this book, chances are good that most interviews will go fantastically. Some conversations will just be good. And others will be absolutely amazing. In general, you're probably going to get great results.

Still, self-doubt can linger and erode your confidence.

You can increase your confidence and the likelihood of great interviews by growing into a few basic mindsets that will help you succeed as a podcast host who conducts interviews.

Follow up with guests that you have interviewed and save their contact information.

What happens when a great podcast interview ends? The postproduction begins. Normal podcasting guides will tell you that this involves editing, audio mixing, writing show notes, and curating additional resources and content.

But there are other post-interview steps that should be taken.

Because you interviewed a person, you have engaged with them deeply and should seek to continue that relationship as a fellow professional in your network. There are a variety of steps you can take to make sure you keep communication open with the people you interview so that if future opportunities to exchange value surface, they can be pursued.

Launch your podcast in less than ninety days from today.

Once you have…

- Adopted the role of interviewer with confidence;
- Written down a podcast concept with a description and have a target listener in mind;
- Created a flexible podcast structure;
- Listed people you want to interview;
- Invited twenty or thirty people to be interviewed on your podcast;
- Organized an inexpensive virtual studio that will allow you to record interviews;
- Recorded five or six interviews utilizing effective practices in interviewing;

… you are ready to launch your podcast.

Following a simple road map, you can take action over the next ninety days and turn the idea of having a podcast into a reality. Imagine your show, where you interview world-class professionals, available on major podcast directories such as

Spotify, Stitcher, Apple Podcasts, Audible, and Google Podcasts. The process is easier than you might think. If you follow the advice in this book and take action consistently, you will have a professional and engaging podcast in three months or less.

You can rapidly grow your sphere of influence at any stage of your career when you launch a podcast that fosters authentic conversations with significant people in your niche, field, or industry. Hosting an interview podcast means directly engaging with the people behind the community you want to serve. And when you make real connections with people in the community, you will be expanding your relevance in powerful ways.

CHAPTER FOUR:

Become a Courageous Interviewer

"I thought I would shake it up a little bit tonight, do something different," she said.

"I'm usually the one asking the questions, but I recently was emailed by Derek, the host of Jazz and Blues Affinity, and asked to do an interview… At first I was a little bit apprehensive about it, but as the interview went on, I felt more comfortable. He has that way."

My interview with jazz vocalist and radio host Stephanie Patton is a highlight of the forty-plus podcast interviews I've conducted. I was honored that she aired a recording of it on her own radio program, *After Hours Alaska.*

What made our conversation so memorable? The answer is simple. We made an authentic and meaningful connection. We discussed the challenges we both faced interviewing jazz musicians, our shared beliefs about the vast possibilities of human potential, and how listening was crucial not just in conversation but in relationships, artistic expression, education, spirituality, and other areas of the human experience.

Before leaving the Zoom meeting, Stephanie told me, "I feel like I've made a new friend." And she had. We had known each other for months as Facebook friends. But it wasn't until we sat down for an hour and talked about an area of mutual interest that we initiated a relationship and connected as peers in the fields of mass communication and jazz advocacy.

Interviews are a process of connection through conversation. If you can ask intentional questions as the host of an engaging podcast, and respect diverse perspectives, you will forge authentic connections and grow your professional network in a way that the thinkers, doers, and achievers of your community will perceive as valuable.

Your mission, should you decide to accept it, is to fully adopt the role of interviewer. Grow into the role. Get excited about it. If you can see yourself owning that role, you will take the first steps toward becoming a successful podcast host.

Start seeing yourself in that role today.

Maybe you are like me. Perhaps sometimes you stutter or stumble over your words. Occasionally, you might overthink your ideas, and they come out as a jumbled mess of sentences that do not feel connected. These factors should not hold you back from stepping into the role of the interviewer, adopting the title with confidence, and growing the skills that underpin effective and engaging question-asking.

Getting practice conducting interviews does not make you perfect. (There is no such thing as perfect.) But it makes you better. And it expands your confidence.

For now, just feel confident as you realize that interviewing is an innate skill you have already been developing all your life. Yes, that's right. You are already an interviewer because you already ask questions! Think about conversations you have had.

For example, if you are like most people, you make some small talk. And questions help you connect with others. When you walk into work, you might make a statement about the weather: "It sure is hot out there today!" When they affirm that it is, you might edge in for a connection that is a little more personal by asking, "So how is that new dog working out?" This provides an opportunity for information exchange, but more importantly, you are connecting to somebody based on something that is relevant to their life.

Every day, you ask questions from all sorts of perspectives and with various intentions. People who learn how to leverage the art of asking questions can engage the people of their favorite online or offline communities in a way that is respectful, thoughtful, and valuable.

Let's take a step back and define "interview."

One of *Merriam-Webster*'s online dictionary definitions states that it is "a meeting at which information is obtained (as by a reporter, television commentator, or pollster) from a person."

This definition is limited, but it is a good start for our purposes. Important points to note:

- Interviews are meetings that happen in a "space."
- An information exchange happens.
- The conversation is perceived as "high stakes" because statements are being recorded and will be shared with audiences via mass communication channels.

What does this mean for the podcast host? Each time you schedule an interview, the guest takes time to meet with you in a space—not just virtually in a Zoom meeting room but also psychologically in the conceptual space of your podcast and its big idea. When you ask them questions, and they answer, you engage in value exchange. And both you and your guest may feel varying degrees of pressure knowing that the conversation is a recorded one and that statements made will be shared in a podcast episode you publish for the world to consume and comment upon.

Information is the basis for an interview. But connecting with people, and drawing out their unique perspectives, should be your focus.

When discussing *60 Minutes*, Don Hewitt once said, "I don't care about issues… I care about how people are affected by the issues."

You should also care about the people.

Behind every niche is a community where you will find different kinds of thinkers, doers, and achievers. You want to ask these people about issues that matter in your field. But you want to help listeners better understand these issues by drawing out your guest's specific perspective. These interviews are fun to listen to. And they also create a connection between you and your guest.

You may wonder, "Why do people meet virtually or in person for high-stakes information exchanges (interviews) often with people they don't even know?"

Researchers from Harvard University published a paper in 2017 analyzing a handful of studies they had conducted about question-asking as a conversational behavior. What is really going on when two or more people start talking?

These researchers discovered that question-asking plays a crucial and underappreciated role in building rapport, connection, and understanding between two individuals. Specifically, they concluded:

"When one conversation partner was instructed to ask many… questions, their conversation partners liked [the] high question-askers more than they liked the low question-askers… In addition to being better liked, participants who were assigned to ask more questions also learned more about their partners. These results show clear benefits to asking questions for both the question-asker and the question recipient… It seems being asked questions increased self-disclosure, which increased liking. These results suggest that people may like question-askers because they enjoy talking about themselves and their own perspectives."

They concluded that question-asking even increased liking in what the researchers described as "high-stakes" conversational contexts, such as a person on a date seeking an intimate relationship with somebody of the opposite sex. In the study they analyzed, those who were asked more questions found their inquisitive potential romantic partners to be more attractive.

Researchers from Harvard University invested a lot of time and expense to confirm what Dale Carnegie wrote several decades ago: "You can make more friends in two months by becoming interested in other people than you can in two years by trying to get other people interested in you." By hosting a podcast where you talk to others, you create a space in which you can be interested in other people and express it through thoughtfully asked questions and authentic conversations.

Interviews are a hidden gem as far as networking is concerned. When we think of all the important elements of networking—initiating contacts, building rapport, finding areas of mutual interest—that's what interviews accomplish. They give you the opportunity and the space to make connections with the world's greatest thinkers, doers, and achievers.

The kind of people we associate with the word "interviewer" is expanding as more people create content for podcasts, blogs, social media, and other forms of new media. But we can learn important lessons about interviewing from professionals who embodied the role in traditional media. Journalists are an example of traditional communication professionals who have valuable insights to share about conducting interviews.

Dean Nelson, longtime journalist, educator, and author of *Talk to Me: How to Ask Better Questions, Get Better Answers, and Interview Anyone Like a Pro*, writes that interviews can be bothersome and even pose risks to interviewees. Yet the people you interview ultimately find the process to be beneficial.

As Nelson explains, “You are an intrusion in their lives, you're the one poking your nose in their business... you're the one staring at them in silence while they try to contain, explain, or compose themselves,” but that when all is said and done, “they're thanking you. Because you listened to them. You asked good questions... You showed interest in their perspective."

As a veteran of journalism who has interviewed a variety of people, Nelson knows instinctively what the researchers at Harvard University confirmed. You build significant connections with people when you demonstrate interest in their perspectives by asking them questions and by giving them a comfortable space to talk about themselves.

Consider the similarities between you as a podcast host and a journalist who interviews people to help flesh out a story:

- You intrude on somebody else's life. Nobody got up today and felt like being on your podcast, especially if it is somebody who does not even know you.

- You are going to be nosy—in a respectful and appropriate way. When you seek somebody else's perspective, you must be interested in their story. Sometimes this can feel awkward unless you are really nosy, like me, in which case this probably isn’t a problem.

- You will be asking the interviewee to enter a high-stakes conversation. Every recorded interview feels like a potentially dangerous conversation for the person being interviewed. It is important to follow best practices that help you put your interviewee at ease and make them feel comfortable with sharing themselves throughout the conversation. Even when the interviewee feels comfortable, they will often pause and stumble when they've been asked a question that causes them to go deeper into their perspective. Sometimes, silence during an interview will intimidate you even more than it does the person trying to formulate an answer.

And yes, most interviewees WILL thank you for interviewing them despite the challenges and awkwardness that the interview poses.

When you follow the steps to set up an authentic space for conversations, and you use effective preparation and recruitment techniques, you will connect with guests in a way that truly values them as people and respects the perspective they have cultivated.

Your podcast space provides guests with value because it gives them a tangible platform on which to share themselves and because they experience psychological benefit when you give them an opportunity to share their perspectives.

When one recognizes the amazing networking opportunities that exist in podcasting, it is no wonder that podcast hosts are using the interview format to create engaging content that audiences want to hear while also forging connections with top thinkers, doers, and achievers in a given niche.

What does it take to create a good podcast interview?

Lawrence Grobel, who has conducted dozens of lengthy interviews with high-profile guests, might have put it best when he said that ". . . a good interview involves many skills: One must be able to converse like a talk show host, think like a writer, understand subtext like a psychiatrist, have an ear like a musician, be able to select the best parts like a book editor, and know how to piece it together dramatically like a playwright."

Suffice it to say, interviewing is not easy.

But the skills we learn through interviewing help us connect with the people in our community and can actually enhance a lot of the other work we do in our careers. We are going to boil down Grobel's colorful job requirements for conducting interviews into three basic skills:

- Listening
- Talking
- Analyzing

Become eager to grow your skills in all three of these areas. Throughout this book, we will cover some strategies, techniques, and best practices that will help you apply these ideas in the context of interviews. But the more you make these skills natural parts of your life and communication style, the easier it will be for you to apply the ideas that underpin good conversations.

Here are some basic ideas to get you started:

- **Listening**. You want to practice active listening skills. Put your focus on the speaker and what they are saying. Don't simply think about what you are going to say next. Grow empathetic listening skills by trying to "hear" what the person is communicating from their perspective based on the situations and challenges they have experienced.

- **Talking**. You must become increasingly comfortable, confident, and skilled with your voice. You also must be able to communicate ideas clearly and with color. These are skills that you grow into over time and through practice. Above all, be authentic. Remember to engage the other person with your words. Prepare questions to ask your guest but be prepared to depart from what you've rehearsed and interact thoughtfully and authentically when in a conversation.

- **Analyzing**. Part of listening and talking is analyzing. But there is also the analyzing that comes before and after an interview. Pre-interview analysis usually involves considering whether or not somebody is a good fit for your show, thinking about an angle from which to ask questions, and preparing some questions to ask based on research you have done. Post-interview analysis involves editing your audio—ethically pruning out pieces that are boring without altering the speaker's message—and composing useful show notes.

You will spend a lifetime getting better at listening, talking, and analyzing. But the time to take on the role of interviewer is today. And as an interviewer, you can begin taking action right now to create your own podcast space where you can interview top-notch guests.

Think back to the story I shared at the beginning of this chapter. Could I have expressed myself better when I interviewed Stephanie Patton? Yes. Were there moments where I could have listened more carefully and perhaps formulated better follow-ups? Sure. Could I have edited the final interview into a tighter finished product? No doubt. But the reason the interview happened was because I took action.

Think of these areas as places for lifelong improvement. Practice them in your daily life and grow into them.

But start right now by deciding to take on the role of interviewer. As an interviewer, you will need a space to have conversations with awesome guests. That is what we are going to work on in the next chapter.

Action Steps:

- Mindsets are the foundation for everything. So write down the following: **I am a podcast host who talks to people in [your niche] because I am passionate about better understanding the people and perspectives behind [your niche].**

- Immediately make a list of ten to twenty people you would like to talk to for one hour. You can include celebrities in your niche whom you've never met, as well as people who already know of you and even preexisting friends and colleagues. Also, consider "Why do I want to talk to these individuals?" What do you find interesting about their perspective as it relates to your niche?

- Cultivate an attitude of curiosity. When interviews go off the rails or fail to ignite, it is usually because the interviewer tries to fit another person's perspective into their own perspective. Be strong in yourself, but also be curious about perspectives that are different than yours.

- Practice clearer speech and conversations in everyday life. Focus on being more present and engaged in all of your social interactions, and podcasting will become easier.

- Listen to quality podcasts. Consider what they are doing. What do you like? What don't you like? This can help you envision your own podcast episodes and will help prepare you for thinking effectively about some of the postproduction choices you will make after you've recorded your first interview.

- Consider interviewing an asset to your personal brand and consistently work on improving how you ask questions. Study interviewers. Observe conversations. Study what is happening when meaningful dialogues are taking place in the media or in your personal life.

CHAPTER FIVE:

Build an Engaging Space for Interviews

"I'm still here… I'm still trying." It was one of the last things he ever said on his podcast.

Let me tell you about a podcaster who we will call Dave. He had everything people say you need to create a good podcast: an engaging speaking style, creative angles for some of the episodes, interesting ideas. As a professional voice-over artist, some episodes even had the kind of crystal-clear audio quality that could rival what you might hear on a professional radio show.

Dave wrote a popular book about how to do podcasting. Without revealing its title, if one were to go to Amazon, they would still find it available in print, e-book, and audible versions. It has well over one hundred positive reviews.

Despite getting many things right with his podcast and even writing a useful how-to book on the topic, Dave's own podcast died after only fourteen episodes. What did he get wrong?

- He made his name and personal brand forefront and center of the podcast's title and concept. Sure, lots of podcasters do this, and you can pull it off too. But the hosts of these personality-centric shows often build an audience BEFORE entering the podcasting sphere.

- He expressed the big idea of his show as being "inane ramblings" about writing, publishing, "coffee, and whatever else." Inane ramblings about broad topics such as writing and publishing? From a total stranger on the internet? No thanks. Nobody has the time.

- He sort of identified his niche. But it wasn't clear exactly what his angle was in the field of writing and publishing. A target audience (or potential interviewees) would not be captivated by the vision of this podcast.

Top professionals in podcasting know that poorly thought-through podcasts are a recipe for frustration and wasted resources. Eric Nuzum, who developed successful NPR podcasts such as *Invisibilia* and *TED Radio Hour*, advises eager new podcasters that the most important pieces of advice he can offer are "Know what you're making" and "Stick to it."

As Nuzum states, "Everything needs to be about something. The best things are about something that is evocative and irresistible. Those best things articulate a vision that's compelling and clear. And the best of the best stick to that vision like it is dogmatic gospel."

The tricky part is to define that special "something."

Your "something" is ultimately a journey of discovery. You will tighten and adjust your podcast concept as it grows and develops, as you get feedback, and as you grow in experience as a host and producer. Our goal in this chapter is to get you off to a solid start so that you will be taken seriously as a podcast host. When you are taken seriously, you can start booking top guests.

First things first. How many different types of podcasts are there, and what kind are you making?

Eric Nuzum claims that there are ONLY two kinds of podcasts: the kind where people chat and the kind where people tell stories. Of these two types of podcasts, there are six varieties. Those are as follows:

- Rant: The podcast host monologues about an idea or opinion.
- Q&A: One person asks questions, another answers.
- Conversation: Less of a long-form interview and more of a discussion between peers.
- Seasonal narrative: A story unfolds over multiple episodes.
- Episodic narrative: One story unfolds during one episode.
- Multiple narratives: Several stories unfold in one episode.

Nuzum does a good job breaking down the categories. If you follow the advice in this book, your podcast is mostly going to be "Q&A" or "Conversation" style episodes.

As your show grows and you develop your own voice and ideas, you may consider branching out and doing occasional

"Rant" episodes. This will help your audience gain a better understanding of your own personal brand. For example, entrepreneur and podcaster Jason Linett hosts a podcast called *Work Smart Hypnosis*. He does conversation-style episodes with significant people in the hypnosis industry. But he also does episodes without guests. In these episodes, he teaches about a topic of significance. *Work Smart Hypnosis* is a great example of a podcast concept that uses multiple episode forms.

Some interview podcasters tightly edit interviews and include a good deal of narration with snippets of interview content to bring depth to a story being told. *Philly Who?*, a podcast by Kevin Chemidlin, uses this strategy to tell the story of Terrill Haigler, a local sanitation worker in Philadelphia during the COVID-19 pandemic. His episode combined scripted narration with more spontaneous interview audio. The results are impressive because you get the emotive content of the interview combined with a more solid narrative that people consume with the same excitement as they would any story. These podcasts take a lot of work. I have been experimenting with this format, but I did not get started this way. I recommend not doing this strategy if you are new to podcasting.

To get started, simply focus on the Q&A structure of asking questions of your guest. Your guest is the focus. Before the interview, you prepare to probe their perspective with thoughtful questions. Think of yourself as playing the role of a journalist in your niche.

Every Q&A podcast provides a unique space for guests to talk about themselves. As the host, it is your job to define the space effectively. Start this process by taking the following steps:

- Define your niche.
- Define how it matters to your personal brand.
- Identify who should care about the podcast.
- Identify where listeners spend their time, money, and energy.
- Consider what problems your podcast addresses.
- Build an avatar.
- Create an elevator pitch.

Research published by Statista in 2018 studied the listening habits of podcast fans in Denmark. Their findings help shed light on why people quit listening to podcasts. The three top reasons are uninteresting topics, too many advertisements, and bad hosts. Uninteresting topics and bad hosts are both likely the result of 1) failing to project your podcast vision or 2) not creating episodes that deliver on the vision that is projected in the podcast description/title/artwork.

You will be much more compelling to potential guests when you make the effort to define your podcast clearly and effectively. Ready to begin? Let's start the process:

Define your niche.

What are you wanting to conduct conversations about? Many podcast hosts create "variety shows" where you talk to all sorts of guests on a wide range of topics. A better strategy, if you want to build your sphere of influence in a specific niche, is to pick only one topic to focus your podcasting efforts on.

You can always create more podcasts later if you feel compelled to talk with guests in other fields.

Selecting one niche makes you focus your efforts. It positions you to be taken more seriously by potential guests and will help you gain a steady audience more quickly.

Define how your niche matters to your personal brand.

What is your relationship to your niche?

One of my niches is jazz music. When I decided to do *Jazz and Blues Affinity*, I could have approached my relationship to the niche in several ways. For example, I studied piano for two years and learned how to play jazz standards such as "Here's That Rainy Day" and "Ain't Misbehavin'." I could have branded myself as a musician related to the field of jazz through the performance of music.

Except I'm not that great of a musician.

I don't know much about improvisation. I've never performed professionally. And I don't have a burning passion to express myself musically like I do through other forms of expression.

Therefore, it made more sense to emphasize my relationship to jazz and blues another way. I approach my guests and audience as an advocate of the music.

Because I work in the self-help industry, I am uniquely interested in the relationship between a person's perspective and what they create. Also, as an advocate, I can rely on my strengths as a historian, as a passionate fan of the music, and as an enthusiast who loves to learn about contemporary artists.

Emphasizing my relationship to the music as an advocate rather than a musician positions me to be taken more seriously as a podcast host. It also positions me to build my personal brand as a thought leader in my niche.

Rely on your strengths. Think about your goals. What impact do you want to make in your sphere of influence? What role are you currently playing? When you define how your niche matters to your personal brand, you are better positioned to think strategically about your podcast concept.

Stop what you are doing. Get out a piece of paper and a pen, and write down the following, filling in the blanks:

My niche is ___________, and my role in this field is that I am ____.
I am interested in this topic because ____________________
____

Here is an example:

My niche is ***jazz****, and my role in this field is that I am* ***an advocate for musicians of this genre****. I am interested in this topic because* ***I am a professional in the self-help field, and I'm curious about the relationship between a jazz artist's perspective and what they create as an artist.***

Other examples could be:

- My niche is dog care, and my role in this field is that I am a veterinarian with over twenty years' experience helping dog lovers keep their pooches in great physical shape. I am interested in this topic because I have loved the companionship that dogs provide me and my clients.

- My niche is video game design, and I am currently in college studying the fundamentals of creating engaging virtual realities that consumers love. I am interested in this topic because I have always loved how engaging online games bring people together and create community.

- My niche is fiction writing, and my role in this field is that I am a mystery novelist. I am interested in this topic because I am a lifelong student of the conventions and classics of the whodunit genre.

These are simple examples. But notice the pattern. You state what your overall topic is going to be, and you define your relationship to that topic.

Identify who should care about the podcast.

You know your niche. You have identified your relevance to it, and this will help you define what kind of space you are creating for conducting interviews.

Now think about what types of people are interested in your space.

Podcasting is an opportunity to grow your sphere of influence, not just through networking but also by building a community around your show. Who benefits from listening? When you are first brainstorming, make the list as long as you like!

List down every type of person who might enjoy your podcast.

For *Jazz and Blues Affinity*, the group of people I started targeting when I first began was music educators. I felt that they would be the most interested in the relationship between an artist's perspective and their action-taking/artistic pursuits.

Narrow down the list you brainstormed until you have one group of people who you think will be the ideal fit for your audience.

Identify where listeners spend their time, money, and energy.

Once you have an idea of who is listening to your podcast, start exploring where they spend money, time, or energy. Good ideas to get you started:

- What books are they buying from Amazon?
- What Facebook groups are they spending time in?
- What are the other online communities in which they participate?
- What do they subscribe to? What magazines, Patreon creators, membership sites, etc.?

Look at what media and information are relevant to your potential listeners right now. This will help you gain a deeper understanding of your niche and potential audience. It will position you to ask better questions and thus help you to be more relevant to your niche.

Consider what problems your podcast addresses.

Think about the needs of your listeners. Ultimately, this is what makes a niche relevant to any audience. People group into niches when they share similar needs and face the same problems.

I have found that podcast hosts often struggle when thinking about needs. I also struggle with this sometimes. For me, a game-changing educational moment was when I read Donald Miller's *Building a Story Brand.* It was written for business owners. But the ideas can be applied by any podcast host who wants to create awesome interviews for a podcast show.

The premise of his book is that people are living a story. They are experiencing a hero's journey.

We engage with brands when they help us be the hero of our story. We can only be heroes when we are empowered to solve problems. Therefore, good brands help us solve problems.

Miller defines three types of problems; those being 1) external, 2) internal, and 3) philosophical. What does this mean? For us, that means that people are motivated to consume podcasts when the content empowers them to solve problems that;

1) Challenge them externally
2) Frustrate them internally
3) Threaten their worldview

Interviews directly or indirectly touch on problems that are important to your listeners and potential guests. What problems exist for the people in your niche? There are two ways of uncovering problems. One way is to identify what is causing pain. The other way is to consider the desires of your listeners.

Identify pains by asking these questions:

- What are the roadblocks to the self-actualization of goals, dreams, and plans?
- What are resources that your audience lacks?
- What are they confused about?
- You can also consider desires. Ask these questions:
- What goal are they trying to manifest as it relates to their niche, and what tools can equip them for their journey?
- What is their passion, and when do they experience the joy of it?
- What are eye-opening ideas, strategies, tips, or facts that could broaden their mind and create a sense of awe as it relates to your niche?

Think about a dog owner's podcast. Who cares about taking care of a dog? People who are motivated by pains and desires. Dog owners experience internal pain when their pet is sick, suffering from pain, or dying a premature death. Some dog owners think (or certainly feel) that it is morally wrong for a person to NOT provide aid to a suffering animal. If they learn tips about how to better take care of their dog, they will feel as if they are better equipped to help their pet live life to the fullest. The dog will thus provide the kind of committed companionship which only a four-legged friend can provide.

Do you see how both pain and desire can be powerful forces in any niche?

Pain and desire define what issues and conversations matter. Even when we are listening to interviews that discuss "other people," we need to think about how the conversation relates to pains or desires experienced by audience members who crave to be the heroes in their own personal journeys.

Build an avatar.

I remember the first time I built an avatar. It was for a marketing class I took while pursuing my bachelor's degree. I was so confused. Exactly how was I supposed to create "one person" that represented an entire segment of a given market?

When you create engaging content, you are not speaking "to the masses." You want to talk to a specific person. Your avatar represents that specific person. Building and refining an avatar helps you to make better choices when conducting, editing, and presenting interviews.

Remember when you identified a group of people who might enjoy listening to your podcast?

Your mission is to take that group and create a fictional person who represents that audience. Here is an example of a podcast avatar I created early on while developing the concept of *Jazz and Blues Affinity*:

This is Jacob. He's thirty-two and married, living in Chicago. He works in a music store and bolsters his income by teaching students trumpet and piano. He has a bachelor's degree in music performance from Berklee. When he was a teenager, he wanted to start his own blues band after falling in love with B.B. King records. While in college, he became interested in the sophistication of jazz. He listened to records by the likes of Charlie Parker, Duke Ellington, and Miles Davis. Jacob believes there is something magical about the creativity of jazz and blues legends. He likes a wide range of music too (he's not snobbish) and enjoys sharing his love of great artists over a beer with friends on the weekends. He thinks "artist" is one of the coolest kinds of professionals in a world of many careers. He found out about Derek's podcast because a musician he loves was interviewed for the show. After listening to that episode, he became interested in Derek's idea of the "Inner Artist," and he likes how his questions bring out inspirational insights from a diverse range of creatives within the jazz field.

My avatar has evolved. And it will continue to evolve.

Start with something. Don't expect to have a fully developed avatar right away. It is a process of discovery that will be aided as you research your niche, cultivate your personal brand, conduct interviews, and gain feedback from actual listeners.

Are you really struggling with this? If so, make YOURSELF the avatar. What do you love about your niche? What are the problems you face? Create a fictional character who mirrors your own interest in the genre. You may attract some like-minded folks, and your content will likely be sharp enough to get some traction so that you can begin pitching guests and getting feedback from listeners.

Another great way to start developing your avatar is to get on Facebook and check out the groups related to your niche. Interact with people. Exchange value. Get to know the people you want in your audience and cultivate a deep understanding of what challenges they face in terms of external, internal, and philosophical problems.

Create an elevator pitch.

Hopefully, you have started thinking about;

- What your niche is and how it is relevant to you.

- Groups of people who should like your podcast.
- At least one avatar who represents one group of people who should like your podcast.

Got all of this? Awesome. You are now ready to create your elevator pitch.

Basically, imagine you are on an elevator. Somebody asks you about your podcast. What do you say? When I created my first elevator pitch, it was this:

Weekly interviews where musicians (and advocates of the music) share personal stories, feelings, and inspirational insights. Gain a deeper affinity for jazz and blues music by discovering the people and perspectives behind it.

Not bad. It gives people an idea of what I do, and several potential guests took it seriously. Because of this pitch, I was able to interview them, and they became fans of what I was doing in my niche.

But eventually, I created a more compelling elevator pitch:

Inspire your inner artist and enrich your understanding of the artist's journey. Join Derek Zboran for interviews that explore the stories and insights of artistically empowered people in the jazz and blues community.

Do not be afraid to get started with something simple, and then let it evolve as you research, interact with the community of your niche, and talk to people who are like your avatar. Also, let yourself work on this process over multiple days. This part of the process requires hard creative work.

If you want a show that rapidly grows your sphere of influence, you must have a solid foundation from which to work.

Completing the steps in this chapter will help you to avoid podfading with inane ramblings, like Dave's podcast about marketing, publishing, and coffee. Work through the exercises in this chapter, and you will be equipped to create a solid podcast concept that will engage listeners and potential guests for years to come.

Action Steps:

- Work through every step listed in this chapter. When you get stuck, take a break and then come back later. Do research. Ask yourself questions. Embrace this process of discovery as an opportunity to learn rather than as a chore.

- Organize all your notes and research during this process into a folder or binder. You are going to likely write and rewrite your avatar, elevator pitch, and lists of pains and desires. You will want to keep this material handy so that you can continuously build on it.

- Ask fellow podcasters for advice on your elevator pitch—and evaluate it with caution. A lot of podcasters are quick to give advice, and you can learn from critiques. But often, your peers tell you everything that is wrong about your podcast. It is easy to fall into the trap of being discouraged and doubting that you have anything worth sharing.

CHAPTER SIX:

Create a Structure for Your Interview Podcast

Recently, a popular musician from Singapore reached out to me online and asked for feedback on her interview podcast. Like one of my own podcasts, *Jazz and Blues Affinity*, hers was a show in which she engaged other musicians in conversations. She wanted to know how to make her show better. I began listening. It wasn't long before I knew what her show needed.

Her interview content was pretty good. She came equipped with good questions and good guests. The area for immediate improvement wasn't in the interviews themselves but rather in how she was delivering that content. The episodes needed more structure.

Podcasts are "shows." And if you think of your favorite show on either radio or television, you will notice that they don't merely provide you with content. They deliver that content with structure.

One mistake a lot of new podcasters make is they simply click record, do a monologue or interview, and then upload the resulting audio file to podcast directories with no editing. When people do this, they are creating audio files, not podcast episodes. Structure helps the listener feel as if they are entering a special place when they click the "Play" button.

As of 2019, about sixty million American households listened to podcasts. That said, most podcasts typically lose 20 to 35 percent of listeners within the first five minutes. I was recently talking to a friend about her podcast listening habits. She told me that she often downloads a podcast that looks promising and "has a cute logo" but turns it off in disgust when it rambles on for minutes without going anywhere. She even told me that a podcast with a great logo (but unfocused content) makes her feel upset. Like many listeners, she hates when a podcast shows potential but fails to deliver on its vision.

There is an easy way to format an interview podcast that will help each episode stay focused, engaging, and worth the listeners' time. When you create a simple and organized structure for your podcast episodes, your show will sound more professional, the episodes will be easier to produce, and you will be better equipped to wow potential guests!

What's the format? It's simple:

- Tell your audience what you're going to talk about.
- Insert a professional introduction that transports people into your interview space.
- Provide the interview.

- End with a CTA (call to action) and/or conclude with a professional outro.

You don't have to follow this structure to call yourself a podcast host and producer. But having this structure makes you sound professional. And listeners enjoy this basic format.

Let's go through each part of this podcast structure;

Tell your audience what you're going to talk about.

This is what opens your podcast episode. This shouldn't be longer than thirty to sixty seconds. In a couple of sentences, simply tell your listeners who you are interviewing and what valuable ideas or opinions they will be discussing during the conversation. Example:

Welcome to Episode #2 of the Jazz and Blues Affinity podcast. Today we have Ray Gallon on the program to talk about finding his own voice as an artist and the value of mentors and teachers in jazz.

They can be a little bit longer, but not by much. Here's one of the longest I have ever done:

This is Episode #8 of the Jazz and Blues Affinity podcast. We are joined today by Ben Golder-Novick, who talks about his recent last-minute gig at Madison Square Garden with the Dave Matthews Band. He also talks about the importance of teamwork in harnessing a synergy of confidence, creativity, and excellence in music performance.

You can get more creative if you want to hook your audience with this introduction. But don't make it too long. Keep it simple. When people click "Play" on your podcast, they think there might be something of value. Your job is to introduce that value quickly so that they keep listening.

Insert a professional introduction.

You want to follow this brief introduction by fading into some music which you license specifically for your show, as well as a professional introduction that introduces your podcast. You will play this introduction for EVERY podcast episode. It is like the theme song of your favorite television show. The music and narrated words become a part of the identity of your program.

For example, old television shows such as *The Fugitive* tell us this about the protagonist of the show against the backdrop of dramatic music:

Name: Richard Kimble. Profession: Doctor of Medicine. Destination: Death row, state prison. Richard Kimble has been tried and convicted for the murder of his wife. But laws are made by men, carried out by men. And men are imperfect. Richard Kimble is innocent. Proved guilty, what Richard Kimble could not prove was that moments before discovering his wife's body, he encountered a man running from the vicinity of his home. A man with one arm. A man who has not yet been found...

Or we could look at *The Twilight Zone* against the backdrop of mysterious and eerie music:

You unlock this door with the key of imagination. Beyond it is another dimension—a dimension of sound, a dimension of sight, a dimension of mind. You're moving into a land of both shadow and substance, of things and ideas. You've just crossed over into the Twilight Zone.

Television shows (especially older ones that had to be watched at a certain time each week on television) have introductions because they introduce the program to new viewers while also helping to cement a "ritual" that helps people psychologically enter the space of the show.

My podcast introduction simply defines my interview space:

"You're listening to the Jazz and Blues Affinity podcast hosted by Derek Zboran. Each week, Derek interviews a diverse range of musicians who perform this music, as well as writers and researchers who advocate on its behalf. Join in for engaging conversations that highlight the individual perspectives behind today's jazz and blues scene. Here's your host, Derek Zboran..."

I used 1930s-style jazz music to set the atmosphere for the show. Think about what music is going to create the right "energy" for the space in which you conduct conversations.

There are probably some changes I would make to the introduction if I were to redo it today. One day I might go in and tighten it up. But just getting started with a simple couple of sentences that define what interviews you do and who you feature sounds professional. It will impress plenty of potential guests and will help you be taken more seriously by listeners.

There are two important points to know about professional introductions. Firstly, you should shell out anywhere from $25 to $125 to have this professionally recorded by a voice-over artist. Do not skimp on this because it adds a layer of professionalism. It communicates that you are serious about your podcast.

If you use a service such as www.voices.com, you will be able to post a script. People will audition at no charge to you. I submitted my introduction job for *Jazz and Blues Affinity* pledging $125. Within hours, over a dozen quality voice-over artists applied and submitted examples of their recordings of the script I provided. The person I ultimately chose was a professional voice-over artist who recorded everything from video game voices to Papa John's pizza commercials.

I had the finished introduction within twenty-four hours of posting the job.

Secondly, you need to pick good introduction music. Do not use copyrighted music to open your show. Aside from that whole problem with violating copyright law, even if you get away with it at first, it will make you look like a third-rate amateur. You want to license "generic music" that can become part of the identity of your specific show.

There are lots of places you can get awesome instrumental tracks. You can use this music to underlay a podcast introduction. If you decide to pursue a voice-over artist on Fiverr, you might even find one who records your introduction and outro and also mixes in some music too. Regardless of where you choose to license music, be sure that you have permission to use the track in your podcast.

If you pay $60 for a licensed song that you can use over and over and $125 for the podcast voice-over for a professional introduction and outro, you will spend less than $200. Each episode will sound amazing. I know some of you might flinch at the idea of spending some money on a podcast that isn't making money directly. But if you want to be perceived as professional, this cost is one that you don't want to skimp on. Listeners and guests alike will decide how professional you are based on the first few minutes of your podcast. It is worth the investment.

Provide the interview.

Next comes the interview. This is the longest part of your episode.

Do not start by launching directly into Q&A with your guest. After your professionally recorded introduction concludes, take some time to introduce your guest and to frame why he or she is an awesome person to feature on the show.

For example, when I interviewed Ray Gallon, I launched into the interview with the following introduction:

Ray Gallon has performed with the greatest of the greats in jazz, including Ron Carter, Lionel Hampton, Art Farmer, Dizzy Gillespie, Sheila Jordan, and Les Paul. Having played for over thirty years, Gallon is a veteran of the jazz scene in the truest sense of the word. Currently, he teaches music at The City College of New York. After playing several hundred gigs and performing as a sideman on numerous albums, Ray Gallon put out his own album as bandleader titled ***Make Your Move*** *in May 2021. It has received high praise from the likes of Ron Carter and Ahmad Jamal. Today we're honored to have Ray on the program for a discussion about his career in jazz and his journey to recording an album as bandleader. Ray, welcome to the program!*

Pro tip: ALWAYS welcome your guest or ask them how they are doing before you start asking questions. This bit of small talk is a fantastic transition from introduction to interview content. It starts building rapport, which is crucial for the start of an interview.

End with a CTA.

I do not encourage you to seek advertising opportunities with your podcast—not when you first start launching a podcast, if at all. (More on that in a bit.) However, you should leverage your space to promote your podcast or your own online presence.

Examples of things you could ask your audience to do:

- Leave awesome reviews of your podcast on Apple Podcasts.
- Visit your website. Sign up for your email list.
- Follow your social media profiles.
- Check out the show notes for your website.
- Listen to the next episode.
- Check out your book, online course, coaching services, etc.

It is perfectly legitimate to ask listeners to take these kinds of actions that bring them further into your sphere of influence. This allows you to bring more value to them and to get valuable feedback from them, which you can use to improve your show.

Outro.

After delivering a call to action, your final step is to add the outro. When you purchase your introduction, make sure you also get a professional outro that thanks listeners for spending their time with the podcast.

Example of my podcast outro:

Thanks for listening to the Jazz and Blues Affinity podcast. Make sure you're subscribed on your favorite platforms so you never miss one of our exclusive interviews. Learn more about the podcast, find detailed show notes, and listen to previous episodes at www.jazzandbluesaffinity.com. Take care and join Derek next week for another great conversation!

Make sure whoever records your introduction also does your outro. I spent $125 for both the intro and the outro—you should get a package deal recorded by the same narrator.

You can only start growing your sphere of influence with your podcast when you are taken seriously. In the previous chapter, you worked on defining some important basics of your interview space. In this chapter, we continued defining that space by clarifying the structure of each episode. Once you complete the activities for this chapter, you are ready to devote yourself to thinking about recruiting guests and creating awesome content for your podcast.

Action Steps:

- Start listening to podcasts with an ear for design. What is the experience of every episode? How does the podcast producer create the impact of that experience through the structure provided?

- Write a brief introduction and outro for your podcast. Look at the examples from this chapter for inspiration. Also, check out how other podcasts you like introduce and conclude their shows. Remember to keep it relatively short. If your intro and outro are at (or over) 150 words combined, it is probably too long.

- Start thinking about editing. If you follow the advice in this chapter, your episodes are going to be built with at least four different audio files. Consider whether you have the skills to assemble audio files in a program like Audacity or if you should hire a podcast editor to do it for you. We will consider the pros and cons of either option in a later chapter.

CHAPTER SEVEN:

Painlessly Book Guests for Your Podcast

It is not as hard as you might think to get high-profile interviewees on your show.

My first excursion into podcasting was with my dad on a project we called *Show Me Rolla.* We interviewed people from the local community. My dad had long had the idea of doing a website "Highlighting and showcasing interesting people, places, businesses, hobbies, activities, and talents in the Rolla, Missouri area from a human-interest perspective." The idea lay dormant for a long while. One day we decided to resurrect the idea. I had previously conducted an interview with a comic book store owner here in Rolla who had owned the business for decades. I enjoyed this experience immensely. Eventually, me and my dad settled on using a DSLR camera to record interviews with a variety of thinkers, doers, and achievers in our local area.

These interviews felt relatively easy to pitch. Most of the people we were seeking to interview were small business owners who had minimal advertising dollars. A chance to be interviewed meant free exposure with a couple of guys who were highlighting the best elements of the community. Why not participate in such a project? During 2020 and early 2021, we recorded several of these interviews and published them on our Facebook page.

Fast-forward to mid-2021. Here in Missouri, we celebrated our bicentennial year, and libraries were encouraged to make this an important part of their Summer Reading Program activities which were still virtual at this point due to the pandemic. My boss at my library job assigned me to handle this part of the programming—given my interest and previous education in history. I asked her for permission to reach out to several authors. At first, I thought I might get one or two. When all was said and done, I had reached out to twelve well-known authors who had written about topics relevant to the history of Missouri. Ten of them agreed. One did not work out. And another ignored my request.

Among those who agreed were a *New York Times* best-selling author, a historian who has assisted in the making of PBS and The History Channel documentaries, and the seventh annual winner of the prestigious Gilder Lehrman Prize for Military History.

Of course, it was an incredible honor to personally talk with all of these immensely talented and successful folks. But do you know what I discovered after this project concluded?

Pitching local business owners in my corner of rural Missouri was basically the same as pitching world-class professionals. You ask the person for an interview. You follow up professionally when they agree or ask questions about your project. And you "close the deal" by getting the interviewee to schedule a time in their busy schedule for an interview with you.

Because interviews are how you connect with others, you can only grow your sphere of influence when you reach out to guests and pitch them effectively.

In our media-saturated environment, we tend to think of people as "famous" or "not famous." The truth is that fame is probably less important than you think. You can literally reach out to almost anybody you want and ask them for an interview.

True, you might have to deal with gatekeepers, and some guests will not be worth the effort—at least not in the beginning stages of your podcast career. And yes, celebrities like Jimmy Fallon probably will get priority over eager, growing podcast hosts such as yourself.

But you should not consider yourself "out of your league" when pitching world-class guests. Ask with confidence. The worst that can happen is that you will be ignored or declined.

What type of guests should appear on your show?

- People you already know.
- People you kinda know.
- People you do not yet know.

You can (and should) book guests in all three of these categories. You will not get every guest you pitch. But it doesn't take many "Yes" replies for you to fill the content publishing schedule of a weekly or biweekly podcast. And once you show consistency in delivering good interviews, it will become easier and easier to book world-class guests on your show.

How to book people you already know. These folks can be the easiest (though not always) to get on your show. They are usually a bit reluctant. But if you are consistent, remind them of the benefits, and emphasize it will be fun, you can usually get them on board. People to consider include:

- Friends
- Family
- Colleagues

Don't just invite anybody on your podcast. Recruit those who fit the concept of your show and who are relevant to your niche. You can be creative with your angles to make certain guests "work" for your show, but they should be relevant in some way.

How to book people you kinda know. This can be hit or miss. Some folks you sort of know will be scared about being on your podcast. The problem isn't you; it's just that they might not remember you, and they are unsure if the podcast is right for them. When reaching out to them, remind them about how you originally connected, tell them your podcast idea, and briefly highlight why you think they're a perfect fit for your podcast.

How to book people you do not yet know. When I embarked upon the *Missouri Bicentennial Series* podcast for the library, some did not believe that I would get the kind of guests I was seeking. Almost all the guests I recruited were highly successful and were people who I emailed out of the blue.

How do you reach out to people you do not yet know and ask for interviews?

First, consider credibility. Libraries are considered one of the wonders of the world by writers and those in academia. This podcast was a library project. Therefore each pitch I sent had a lot of credibility. Guests could easily see how the project was relevant to their field, and they were happy to participate in the project.

You don't have to work in a library to have credibility. The point is to think about how you have credibility in the eyes of the particular guests who you seek to invite on your show. When I pitched guests for *Show Me Rolla*, my credibility was linked to the fact that I loved the community and was known for doing independently produced media projects that highlighted the best parts of the community.

When I did *Jazz and Blues Affinity*, the credibility was that I was a student of interviewing who loved jazz and wanted to put that growing skill to work for the jazz community.

Think about your strengths. How do you have credibility? Make sure your public social media profiles (and website, if you have one) reflect that credibility. And emphasize that credibility when you pitch potential guests to be featured on your show.

So what guests should you consider booking for your podcast?

If you're starting out, avoid asking mega-famous guests who are surrounded by gatekeepers. This requires a skill set beyond the scope of this book. If this sounds disappointing, consider shifting your focus. It doesn't matter what niche you are conducting interviews in. There are "famous" people who work independently (or mostly so) and who would be happy to talk with you.

Consider some of these suggestions for ideas about where to find guests:

- Who is authoring books about your niche?
- Who is doing podcasts in your niche?
- Who is being featured in major publications in your niche?
- Who is blogging about your niche?
- Who is creating new products in your niche?
- Who is offering services in your niche?

People in these categories would love to appear on a quality podcast. It is your job to provide them with that opportunity.

Hopefully, you are seeing the possibilities for your podcast. Now it is time to take action. Here is the simple step-by-step system you need to start booking guests this month:

1) **Make a list of people you want to interview.**

In chapter four, I asked you to make a list of people you could interview for your podcast. If you haven't done that yet, no worries. But now is the time to get busy. Sit down and make a list of twenty to fifty people who you think would be awesome for your podcast. Do not think small. If a name pops up in your head and they are relevant to your niche, list them down regardless of how famous they are. (Don't only think up famous people, though.)

When you've got a list of fifty people or so, proceed to the next step.

2) Which of these people do you already know or have a connection with?

Do you already know or have some type of connection with any of the individuals on your list? You don't have to be friends with them or know them "well." Maybe you are a connection on a social media site such as Facebook, LinkedIn, or Twitter. Or perhaps you have their email address or phone number. Maybe you have their business card after meeting them at an event somewhere. The point is to circle which folks you already have a connection with, where you might be more likely to have success with an interview request.

Circle everybody you currently know. These will likely be the easiest people to book and can help you get the podcast started. Once you've got it launched, you can reach out to folks you do not yet know.

3) Use the BEST test.

Go through your list of fifty or so people. Now apply what I call "the BEST test." This means for everybody on the list quickly consider if they will…

- Be insightful in a conversational context?
- Establish a connection of relevancy to your audience?
- Share the interview with their own audience?

- Talk with authority, experience, passion, personality, or some other valuable trait?

Extra points if they fulfill the above criteria and you already know them.

4) Get contact info.

Gather contact info for five people you want to start with. Gather social media info and any interesting info about what they do. This means doing a simple Google search; it means looking up their social media profiles and simply finding out what info they (or others) have generated intentionally or unintentionally about their brand.

5) Come up with a working angle.

When you prepare for an interview, most professionals will always think of a basic angle by which to brainstorm possible topics and questions.

Ask yourself, "How might this person be a good fit for my podcast?"

Write two or three sentences about what they do. Describe why you think your audience would benefit from hearing from this person.

Developing a working angle early in the interview process helps you to frame the pitch. It allows you to tell the guest exactly why you think they are a good fit for your show. Doing this kind of thinking illustrates that you are serious about having them on the show.

6) Pitch them on being on the podcast.

Yes, this is the scary part. Type out an email. Proofread it carefully. Then take some action. You must send your pitches if you are going to be successful as a podcast host.

Keep pitches short and simple. Ask for what you want clearly, and briefly let them know why you are asking to interview them. Examples of pitches I have made:

Show Me Rolla requesting to interview a local business owner through Facebook Messenger:

*Hi Kristina! Hope you are having a great holiday season. My dad, Jim, and I recently launched a website/Facebook page called Show Me Rolla. Through video interviews, we are seeking to delve into Rolla from a human-interest perspective. We have recently done interviews with Krista Kelly, the president of the Phelps County Historical Society, and a music instructor over at Merle's Music. If you would be interested in doing an interview related to Kristina's Casa, you can give me a call at 573-***-**** (or just message me back here if you prefer) and we can see about scheduling something for one of our openings in January.*

Missouri Bicentennial Series with the Rolla Public Library, pitching a guest I learned about by doing a search for Missouri-related history books on Amazon:

Hi Chuck! My name is Derek Zboran, and I work as a staff member with the Rolla Public Library in Missouri.

To celebrate the Missouri Bicentennial, the library has been hosting author interviews with a handful of top writers and historians.

Would you be interested in doing a thirty to forty-five-minute virtual interview regarding Charlie Parker? Our conversation will be based on your book, **Bird: The Life and Music of Charlie Parker**.

This will be prerecorded virtually and later broadcast on our Facebook and YouTube platforms.

Over the summer, we did four successful interviews with authors who wrote about Missouri history, including The New York Times best-selling author A. J. Baime and the award-winning military historian John McManus.

Let me know if you're interested in doing the interview, and we can work out scheduling and other details. We are looking for authors for September through December.

Best regards,

Derek Zboran

Jazz and Blues Affinity, requesting interview with an award-winning jazz vocalist:

Hi Angela! I work on virtual programming for a public library here in Missouri. I have done interviews with a variety of authors, including The New York Times best-selling author A. J. Baime and the award-winning author John McManus. I want to put my growing interview skills to work for the jazz community, and I'm doing so with a podcast to be launched in October or November. It will be called Jazz & Blues Affinity, and the idea is that musicians and advocates can share their stories through interviews that encourage expression of unique perspectives and inspirational insights. I would love to interview you for an episode of this upcoming podcast .... Your story of overcoming cancer and pursuing your passion for jazz would be an amazing fit for the podcast I am putting together. Let me know if you're interested. The interviews are fun and conversational and will take no longer than thirty to forty-five minutes.

I crafted these messages at various points in my two years of experience with podcasting. All of them were successful. Were they perfect in every way possible? Nah. But they got the ball rolling, and from there, we scheduled times and recorded awesome interviews.

Why did these requests work? I think it was because I thought about what I would think if I were famous and received a request to be on a podcast.

I would want to know…

- Who is asking?
- Why are you asking me for an interview?
- What is your connection to the topic you want to talk to me about?
- What kind of commitment am I making (in terms of time and technology) if I say yes?

Most of the pitches depicted above covered these four angles.

So as you are crafting your pitch, include the following:

1) Identify yourself. Who are you, and what is your podcasting project?

2) Ask them point-blank. Simply ask them what you want. "Would you be interested in doing an interview for such and such number of minutes regarding topic XYZ?"

Don't take forever to get to your request. People don't have time to read long emails from strangers.

3) Tell them where the podcast will be published; Spotify, Apple Podcasts, Stitcher, etc.

4) Make a statement or two that supports why you are a worthwhile person to talk to. Have you done any previous interviews? Do you have experience in your niche? Are you a student who is eager, humble, and wanting to learn? Think about your advantages and own them with confidence.

5) Specifically ask them to let you know if they want to do an interview. For some reason, in my own experience, concluding the email with "Let me know if you are interested..." seems to have good results. Try it out and see if it works for you!

You can structure the pitch any way you like, but it's a good idea to cover these five areas. Also, if you have a website that features your previous podcast work, include a link to it in your pitch.

Why do people want to do interviews with you?

Pitching is easier when you take the focus off yourself and think in terms of how you are benefiting the other person. Genuinely think in terms of what value you are providing with your podcast project. It will help you feel less nervous. And you'll take both success and failure less personally.

What are the reasons why people go on podcasts?

- They want good content they can share on their social media profiles.
- They want to create momentum around a project, and media appearances help.
- They want to make connections with media-savvy people who take their field seriously.
- They want experience in getting their message out.
- They want to sell something.
- They think it is cool to be on a podcast. (Do not underestimate this benefit!)

All of it revolves around you building a space that others want to be invited into. Think in terms of what value you are providing, and you will have more confidence when you pitch. Remember what Dale Carnegie advised: "You can make more friends in two months by becoming interested in other people than you can in two years by trying to get other people interested in you."

How to consistently increase the number of people you can interview.

If you want to consistently increase the number of people you can interview, the best advice I can give you is to get out where your niche is hanging out. Meet and interact with them.

That means join social media groups. Add value to the communities. The more active you are on social media in a way that contributes value (not just toots your own horn), the easier it will be to find suitable guests to pitch to.

You can only grow your sphere of influence when you reach out to guests and pitch them effectively. Take the following actions to get started.

Action Steps:

- Make or add to your list of people you want to interview. Brainstorm thirty to fifty names. Include a mix of people you know, kinda know, and do not know at all.

- Use the BEST test to evaluate your list. If you are just starting out with podcasting, consider individuals you already have a connection to, as they can be easier to pitch.

- Pick five or six of the names you brainstormed before you move on to the next chapter. Craft a short message asking them to be on your show. Look up their contact info and send them an email or direct message! Get the ball rolling.

CHAPTER EIGHT:

Prepare for Your First Interview

You reach out to twenty or thirty guests from the list you brainstormed in the last chapter. Nothing happens for a few days, maybe even weeks. But then you start getting "Yes" replies. People want to be on your show! What comes next?

I'm embarrassed to admit this, but when I first began reaching out to high-profile guests, I did not actually "know" what to do when guests replied affirmatively to my interview request. Having been through the process dozens of times has helped me figure out some dos and don'ts.

In this chapter, we are going to look at:

- How to follow up with affirmative responses and set up the details of your interview.
- How to prepare effectively for your interview.
- Nine guidelines to help you navigate from the point of getting a "Yes" to the moment you actually start recording an interview.

In the past, I wasted too much time, energy, and frustration on the part of the interview process between getting a "Yes" and doing the interview. When you learn some basic guidelines, you will be equipped to tackle this part of podcasting with ease so that you can focus on growing your sphere of influence.

Setup Details

People will generally reply to an interview request in one of three ways:

- Ignore it. (Yuck.)
- Agree, but ask that the interview be conducted at a time in the future.
- Enthusiastically agree and ask when to set up a time!

Let's assume you've had an affirmative response.

If somebody agrees but asks that the interview be conducted at a time in the future, reach out with a version of the message you see below.

Hi person XYZ!

Thanks for your interest in being interviewed on [my podcast title]!

We can definitely wait to conduct the interview. It's a [weekly/bi-weekly/monthly] podcast, and I do interviews regularly throughout the whole year.

I'll reach out to you again in [suggest a month or number of weeks].

Thanks again. Can't wait to feature you on the podcast when the time is right!

In my experience, the three primary reasons for asking that an interview be conducted in the future are: 1) they think the exposure will be beneficial to a project they are about to finish but are not ready to talk about, 2) they have too many immediate commitments on their plate, or 3) they are ill or dealing with a personal crisis.

Make sure you follow up with the guest when you said you would.

Many guests will enthusiastically agree and ask when to set up a time. This is awesome! Because the quicker you can get your guests booked and interviewed, the better your content publishing schedule will look.

For those who agree, you have to achieve the following objectives:

- **Arrange a time.** Do yourself a favor and use a service such as Calendly to book appointments. When I started podcasting, I would literally send off a list of times and dates and let my guest choose from that list. This has multiple issues. Firstly, it is not professional. Another problem is that you have to wait for them to reply before you know which of those available times are "still available" for other guests. This creates problems if you try to book multiple guests simultaneously.

- **Set expectations around what will be required.** How are you recording the podcast interview? Should they expect a Zoom link or something else? What do they need to do when they get this link? Assure them how easy that part is. Also, you might recommend that they use Google Chrome when they connect to the interview. I had an interview almost get derailed once when somebody attempted to use Internet Explorer to connect to a StreamYard broadcast.

- **Remind them of some best practices that will help them sound great.** Tell them that for best results, they should connect to the interview in a place with high-speed internet, use an external microphone (if possible), wear headphones (more important than you would think), and go to an area that is relatively quiet.

Some interviewees will be totally "chill" throughout the whole process. Once they're scheduled and they know how they will be connecting to the interview, you won't hear from them again until the day of the interview. Others will send you several messages or emails asking for clarification of details.

Either way, if you can get the time arranged and let them know what to expect in terms of connecting, you will be doing everything in your power to ensure a successful interview.

Prepare, Prepare, Prepare

You can successfully interview people for your podcast when you take simple steps to prepare for your conversation ahead of time. How much should you prepare? That depends on several factors, including how much time you can invest, your personal interview style, and your own level of experience.

There appear to be two extremes in research and interview preparation.

On the one hand, some think that doing any research prior to the interview will ruin the "spontaneity" of the conversation. Podcast hosts who preach this extreme defend their actions by claiming it results in better interviews. You will probably hear them say, "I want to be surprised when they answer my questions! I want to ask questions from the point of view of my audience!"

On the other hand, there is the extreme of overpreparation. Such hosts try to soak up every word ever written by—or about—the guest. They scour the internet, read all the books and articles, and study reviews. This group defends their actions by pointing out that most experts suggest that at least some research is important before doing an interview. If some research is good, more research must be better!

My suggestion to you is to take a sensible middle ground. If you need inspiration, look no further than the story of the interviewing legend Terry Gross.

Gross is well known for laser-sharp focus during her NPR interviews. She effortlessly glides from one topic to the next, and she has a natural talent for follow-up questions. If you listen to interviews from later in her career, you are listening to meticulously researched interviews. She also has professionals to help her research every guest that appears on NPR's *Fresh Air*. She also does not have to invest time and energy into literally every aspect of the production of her podcast as you and I do.

But did you know that Gross did not start this way? Her start with interviews involved much lighter research. Eric Nuzum, one of the creative minds over at NPR who helped develop *Fresh Air*, reveals this in his book, *Make Noise*:

"Today on *Fresh Air*, Terry, assisted by a staff of producers, spends hours preparing for each interview: reading a mass of material on each guest, spending time with their work; writing, editing, and rewriting questions, then spending many more hours editing the interview… But cohosting fifteen hours a week back in her Buffalo days with no support staff didn't afford much time for prep… [According to Terry Gross] 'I don't think I was working as hard as I do now to get beneath the surface of things. We didn't have time for that. Some interviews, I could read an article, but that's about it.' In place of research was innate curiosity. 'I always try to clarify in my own mind why this person matters and why it's worthy of our listeners' time.'"

If Gross got started by relying on the research of reading a single article combined with her innate curiosity and the right focus (namely, what value her guests could provide in her interview space), why can't you get started this way?

I'm not going to tell you what "the right" amount of preparation looks like. It is different for every podcast host, topic, and guest.

My best recommendation is to strike a balance between under-preparation and overpreparation. You want to get enough information to structure your curiosity and nurture your sense of what questions are going to be relevant to your audience.

However, as an indie podcaster who is likely managing all (or nearly all) phases of podcast creation, you need to be mindful of your investment of time and energy. Do not burn out of podcasting because you take too long to research your guests.

Here is how I approach the research process for interviews:

- Firstly, consider the why of the interview. Why did you contact this guest? Why is their perspective relevant? How might this guest have a perspective that will help your audience with a problem they have externally, internally, or philosophically (as discussed in Chapter 5)?

- Secondly, find synthesized info. Look them up on Wikipedia. Check out the bio on their website. Get a sense of the person and a rough timeline of their career and activity within your niche.

- Thirdly, now that you have your angle and the big picture view of their life, start researching as deeply as you can. Read the book they wrote. Watch the movie or documentary they directed. Listen to the album they recorded. Scour YouTube for old interviews they conducted. Get to know them as intimately as your time and energy allow. Jot down interesting ideas. Let your "angle" evolve and mature as you get a better idea about why they have a perspective that's of interest to your avatar.

- Fourthly and finally, create a handout for yourself to use as a resource when you interview. This means writing a brief introduction based on your research. Then, list fifteen to eighteen interview question ideas. Consider which questions are going to work best for the guest you have recruited.

Sometimes it is hard to think up good questions. Some of my favorite question ideas include:

- If you could go back in time, when you first started [blank], what advice would you give yourself?
- Why are you passionate about [blank]?
- What are some challenges you have experienced?

Once, I asked members of a popular podcasting group what they routinely asked guests. Here are some of the answers that I received:

- Who do you admire most and why?
- What was your first job?
- If everything goes perfectly on your next project, and someone walks up to you afterward, what do you hope they'll say to you?
- What's one thing people generally don't know about you?

You can get a lot of good ideas by looking at "podcast question lists" that are published online. You can also get ideas by watching or listening to quality interviews. That said, I would use a bit of creativity and customize good question structures based on unique information you learn through your research.

Remember to put this all in a Word document. This will give you the confidence to do a great job. For example, when I conducted my first interview, this was the preparation document I made:

Introduction:

Laurie Dapice is a jazz vocalist based in New York City. In 2006 she graduated with a bachelor's degree in performance and music from The New School of Jazz & Contemporary Music in Manhattan. She has either studied or performed with some of the world's top musical talent, including Wynton Marsalis, the Jazz at Lincoln Center Orchestra, Billy Harper, Barry Harris, Reggie Workman, and Charles Tolliver. In 2015, she independently produced her first album, *Parting the Veil*, which is currently available on Bandcamp. The album won four stars in a DownBeat jazz review written by the late journalist Bob Protzman. The music has been enjoyed by listeners around the world thanks to generous public radio hosts on top jazz radio broadcasts. From initial conception to fruition, the album's arrangements and ideas for production depended almost squarely on Dapice herself. She made key creative decisions when it came to writing out the arrangements, recruiting musicians, cultivating the album's artistic vision, and other crucial elements of producing a well-rounded album. For these reasons, *Parting the Veil* is not just an accomplishment in vocal jazz. It also represents one musician's successful journey into the world of pursuing her own musical ambitions outside the realm of traditional big-name record labels. Today we're honored to have her on the program to talk about how she made her first album a reality.

Questions:

1. Take us into the moment when you first received the copy of your CD, *Parting the Veil*. What did it feel like to hold this album in your hands?

2. You were born in rural New York State in a town called Utica. From there, you migrated to Manhattan and pursued a career as a jazz singer. What was the moment that you realized you wanted to enter the world of jazz as a professional musician?

3. You graduated with a bachelor's degree in performance and music in 2006, and you have studied with a diverse range of significant talent, including Kenneth Kamal Scott, Chico Hamilton, and Amy London. At any point during your education, did you ever have the idea, "You know what, I want to record my own album?"

4. Independently producing a jazz album can be a difficult journey. You did a lot of the legwork on your own, including writing the arrangements, and choosing musicians, and recording vocals. What inspired you to take this route?

5. You finished *Parting the Veil* in 2014 and released it in 2015. But when did the creative work begin on this album?

6. In total, you had ten musicians accompanying you on this album. What are some important ways that these musicians shaped your project?

7. In the liner notes, you write that "While developing a concept for this album, I decided to define something I had lived; the 'veils of matter' that many people experience and live under in their lifetime, that shape, mold, and change us… and what can result from a greater understanding of oneself once those veils are parted..." What does this phrase "parting the veils" mean to you?

8. One of the standouts for me when I first listened to your album was your cover of "Feeling Good" by Nina Simone. It was so different from the original. Did you feel like you took creative risks with some of the arrangements?

9. Originals on this album include "Goodbye Summer" and "Winter Waltz." What are some of the biggest challenges of composing an original in contrast to arranging a standard?

10. Over a decade ago, you posted on your Twitter account, "What you risk reveals what you value…" What risks did you feel you took with *Parting the Veil*?

11. Looking back, what brings you the most joy about having recorded and released *Parting the Veil*?

12. You specifically mention iconic jazz vocalists in your liner notes, including Billie Holiday, Abbey Lincoln, Sarah Vaughan, Anita O'Day, and Ella Fitzgerald. At any point during the making of this album, did these icons inspire you to realize your own goals as a musician?

13. One of the people to who you dedicate the album is your grandmother. You've mentioned to me before on Facebook how important both your dad and son have been to you. What role has family played in your artistic pursuits?

14. Artists and professionals in a variety of fields—not just in the music business—are increasingly empowered to pursue their creative projects independently. What is one lesson you learned that you would share with somebody who wants to pursue a personal vision and independently launch a project such as you did with *Parting the Veil*?

Notice a couple key details:

- It starts with an introduction which I can read. The one I wrote for this first interview is longer than I normally do now. But the point is to write something that you can read aloud when the interview begins that introduces your guest in a positive way.

- There are only fourteen questions (instead of fifteen like I now do and which I recommend). I have found that fifteen to eighteen is an optimal number of questions to brainstorm.

- Research was involved. I took time to set questions up. Furthermore, those questions were asked in a way that reflects deep thought about this artist and her career.

I encourage you to put in some effort when it comes to preparation. You don't have to set up all the questions in the detailed way that I did here. In fact, now that I have more experience, I tend to jot down question ideas with a lot less setup. Regardless of how much work you put in, I encourage you to take the preparation seriously and create a preparation sheet that will give you confidence.

Nine Rules for Arranging and Preparing Interviews

The period between the time you get a "Yes" and the time you actually interview can be a hectic one. Alas, doing an interview-based program is not for the faint of heart. Following these nine simple guidelines will help you feel more confident throughout the process and get better results.

1. **Be courteous and professional at all times.** Remember that every effort your interviewee invests in you and your show is a gift to you and your audience. Treat it as such.

2. **Communicate with brevity.** You don't need to ramble on about "lots of this and lots of that" when you are trying to arrange the details of an interview. Be friendly and do not waste the time of your guest who has to add an interview to all their other stressors.

3. **Provide a list of interview topics and avoid showing exact questions to guests.** I avoid sending exact questions to guests because I want them to be more engaged in the moment of the interview, and I want them to have more spontaneous interaction. It's okay to send a list of broad topics (six to eight) that give them a good idea about where you will take the conversation. This is not a hard-and-fast rule for me; if the guest insists on a question list, I do provide it.

4. **Do not agree to show the guest your finished episode.** Sometimes guests will ask that you show them the finished episode or may suggest that this would be a good idea. Save yourself a world of frustration. Make it a policy that you do not show guests the edited interview ahead of time. It has been my experience that guests can get nervous and then ask for endless edits. They may even ask you to scrap a whole show that is perfectly awesome because they are worried about how they come off when they responded to a question thirty or forty

minutes into the interview. Release your interview and let your guest hear it along with your audience.

5. **Consider whether or not you are using a release form.** Obviously, this book can't recommend legal advice. All your legal questions should be addressed with a real lawyer. That said, experts state that you do not necessarily need a release form in every interview situation. Furthermore, many podcast hosts do not make all their guests sign a release. Decide if you are going to use one or not and under what circumstances you would. Then make that your policy. Recognize that if you decide to have all guests sign a release form no matter what, you may lose quality guests. Not everybody is keen to sign a release (which often requires them to list their personal address) and submit it to a total stranger online who calls himself a podcast host. Asking for this kind of personal information creates a barrier. However, I do recommend you save emails or online correspondence in which they consent to give you a podcast interview.

6. **Be patient.** Your guest may do things that are annoying. Occasionally they will even be demanding and rude. You can set boundaries if necessary, but you also should remember not to take things personally. Remember, it's just an interview.

7. **Consistently use positive language about what the interview experience will be like**. Ben Golder-Novick, one of the original performers with Postmodern Jukebox, told me in an interview that he feels like he owes it to his fellow band members to not be nervous

when he gets up on stage. Confidence breeds confidence. You owe it to your guests to not be nervous.

8. **Always put the emphasis on the other person.** Take a service-based attitude to how you conduct interviews, and you will feel less nervous. Some journalists think of themselves as public servants, and this habit helps them avoid getting wrapped up in the dramatic news conflicts that they are supposed to be covering in an objective way. Remember, it is not about you. It is about the person you are interviewing and how their perspective is relevant to your field.

9. **Be confident but not arrogant.** You don't need to show off. But you also should be strong in yourself and in the importance of your job as somebody who is probing their perspective.

At this point, you are ready to schedule interviews and prepare for success. Some of you are ready to start recording. Others may be wondering how they are going to conduct an interview from their home office, basement, bedroom, or closet. If that sounds like you, go on to the next chapter, where I'll give you the nontechie's guide to an excellent podcast setup that will help you sound great and record amazing interviews for your podcast.

Action Steps:

- Have you reached out to potential guests yet? Pull out that list you brainstormed and start reaching out! You can only start preparing for interviews after you have successfully pitched a couple of guests. You'll want to have four or five episodes recorded before you launch your podcast. So that means you need to get four or five different guests to agree to appear on your show. Get busy!

- Study quality interviews as well as poorly executed interviews. If possible, watch filmed interviews where you can observe body language. Consider interviewing a craft at which you can get better and better. This will help you prepare for interviews more effectively.

- Start looking for other interviews in your niche. Who is conducting the interviews? What kinds of questions do they have? What kinds of conversations are being created? You should look at what others are doing—not to copy but to help you learn what is working (and what isn't).

CHAPTER NINE:

Record Your Interviews with a Painless Podcast Setup

If you search around online, you will hear about numerous setups for podcasters. You'll read heated debates between audio nerds. You will search through countless lists of podcast microphones with funny names that cost hundreds of dollars. You will be supplied with contradictory advice about what you need and what you don't to produce a professional-sounding podcast.

A fraction of you love exploring podcasting gear, and you're eager to dive into the rabbit holes. The rest of us nontechies just want something that works great and is easy to set up and start using.

I have two rules for beginning podcasters based on my own experience. Record podcasts with a setup that involves 1) minimal expense and 2) minimal learning curves. Once you have started recording episodes and your show starts growing, then you can scale up your setup into something fancier.

There are relatively inexpensive options out there that are affordable and will help you sound great. For this book, I am going to recommend a setup that will work great for shoestring budgets. Some of the equipment you may already own! Basically, I want you to get this part of your podcast journey figured out quickly and painlessly. That way, you can focus on the important part, which is creating interviews and publishing podcast episodes on schedule.

First, let's get started with what you need:

- Computer
- Internet connection
- Virtual recording software
- Web camera
- Microphone
- Headphones

Let's talk briefly about each item you need. Hopefully, as you make your way through this chapter, you feel your confidence increase as you begin to realize just how doable it is to record professional-sounding podcasts on a shoestring budget with the most basic of equipment.

Computer. I recommend setting up a desktop computer. Avoid recording podcasts on a laptop or mobile device such as a phone or tablet. Laptops often operate more slowly than desktops and can have difficulty running multiple applications at one time. You do not have to purchase an upscale computer.

Internet connection. You need high-speed internet to conduct interviews. I used to have the worst internet imaginable, and I shudder to think how I would do my podcast today if I still used such slow internet. Upgrade your internet connection if your current plan doesn't provide what you need. Also, consider connecting your internet through a wired connection directly to your router, as it can help ensure reliable and consistent internet speed.

You need something that I call "the virtual studio." For many of you, this will be Zoom. For others, it will be a service such as StreamYard, Riverside, or SquadCast. Some podcast books warn against using Zoom. However, I disagree. Firstly, Zoom has vastly improved since the 2020 pandemic forced us all online. Secondly, more people than ever before have used Zoom and feel comfortable meeting other people with the platform. Many of the guests you invite on your show will not be tech-savvy. Cut out the stress and overwhelm by inviting them into a virtual studio that they already have experience using successfully.

When you do use Zoom, I suggest recording files locally and separating the tracks. This makes a huge difference when you (or the editor you hire) edit and mix your audio. Every participant in the Zoom meeting should have their own track recorded separately. You can set this as a setting in Zoom.

Web camera. Some podcasters record audio only; others record video. In general, for long-form interviews, I tend to focus more on audio. Regardless, I want a decent-quality web camera. Going into the interview, I have my webcam turned on so I can greet the guest virtually face-to-face.

I have experimented with doing these interviews with cameras on and off. My experience has been that turning the cameras off gets better results.

I find it extremely difficult to look at the camera lens rather than the person on the screen. When this happens, the person on the screen is seeing me look in a different direction which can be awkward.

Also, I have noticed that I just tend to get better audio when I have the guest communicating in an audio-only format. I can focus more intently on the ideas they are sharing, and they are forced to communicate slowly through their voice.

Obviously, if you are doing video too, you would leave your webcam on for the whole duration.

Whether you interview with your web camera on or off, a wonderful device I purchased a bit ago that I have enjoyed using is a Nexigo 1080P. It works great. I can rotate it around, it records me in quality video, and it is relatively inexpensive!

Microphone. And finally, we arrive at the big question. What microphone should you buy?

If you want an option that is incredibly inexpensive and yet stunningly high quality, buy a Blue Yeti. These can be purchased for around $100 and are super easy to set up. All you do is plug the USB into your computer, and you are ready to record.

There are two settings on the back of the Yeti microphone that you should be aware of. One is the GAIN which should be set low.

The other is the PATTERN which determines from what directions the microphone will record sound. Since you are talking into the microphone by yourself at a desk or table, you should set this to the setting that looks like an upside-down heart. This blocks off noise from the back and opens up the device for recording from the front surroundings.

There is a final add-on you ought to consider when it comes to your Blue Yeti microphone; a pop filter. This can be attached to the base of the microphone and adjusted over the mouth section. This is extremely useful because it filters out the plosives, which result in unpleasant pops in recorded audio when you say words like “stop” or “spot.”

Headphones. Wear headphones when you do interviews. Why? Because it means your interviews will sound a lot better. Having conducted over forty interviews, I’ve learned that you need a pair of headphones that are comfortable to wear for an hour. I get the big kind put out by OneOdio.

You likely already have most of what you need, except maybe a microphone and headphones. Everything I mentioned in this chapter can be found with links to Amazon on a special page I created on my website, https://professionalpodcastcreation.com/podcastequipmentforbeginners/

You don’t have to follow the advice in this chapter. But if you are just getting started, I strongly encourage you to give my ideas a try. Everything described is exactly the setup I have used for *Jazz and Blues Affinity*. Truth be told, my previous podcasts have used equipment that was of even poorer quality than I outlined in this chapter. Even with the most rudimentary of tools, I achieved decent results. You can do a lot with basic tools!

Sounding professional is essential if you want to grow your audience and be taken seriously by guests. But that does not mean you have to spend tons of money or buy complicated equipment that will have you swearing like a sailor into the wee hours of the night struggling to set it up. Using the simple suggestions here, you will create an awesome setup that will help you get started quickly and painlessly.

Action Steps:

- Evaluate what you currently have. Remember, to start recording interviews virtually, you need:
    - Desktop computer
    - Internet connection
    - Virtual recording software
    - Web camera
    - Microphone (and pop filter)
    - Headphones

What is on that list that you still need? For a handy checklist with links, go to my website: https://professionalpodcastcreation.com/podcastequipmentforbeginners/

CHAPTER TEN:

The Art of Conducting Quality Interviews

My head had been throbbing all day. Reason unknown. My room was strategically cleaned so that all my clutter was out of the eye of my web camera. Within five minutes of the interview starting, I heard somebody in my household creep into the living room so that they could turn on the noisy television. Hadn't I reminded everybody in the house that I was recording a podcast interview with one of my favorite musicians ever? The audacity!

Meanwhile, on the musician's end, sharp, piercing sounds of metal striking against metal and other objects shot through my headphones as we recorded the podcast conversation. (Didn't do my headache much good.) At one point, it sounded like a steel door had been kicked down.

"You have some noises in the background," I said politely, hoping that the noises might be easy to identify and eliminate for the remainder of the interview.

"Oh yes," she replied. "I'm here in my mom's bakery." And given that we were recording the interview the night before Thanksgiving, it was no surprise that things sounded busy!

This wasn't the first time an interview felt like it was going completely wrong. But do you want to know the funny thing? By the time I did some basic editing, the audio did not sound perfect, but it was good enough. The conversation itself was a lot of fun, and we covered her perspective in quality depth. The edited interview would end up becoming my most downloaded podcast episode to date and nearly placed *Jazz and Blues Affinity* into the top 25 percent of podcasts based on seven-day downloads.

Interviews where you seem to "lose control" and things feel like "they're not working" are sometimes the best podcast interviews you will ever do.

Doing an interview podcast means you have to embrace uncertainty. You literally do not know what is not going to go according to plan. When things go wrong (or seem to go wrong), you will not always be able to immediately fix it. This is simply a mindset that must be adopted.

When you truly embrace the interview process, you recognize that things do not always go according to plan and that you have to record conversations in circumstances that are sometimes less than ideal—especially when you record virtually.

I do not say these things to discourage you. I simply want to put you in the right mindset.

The interview process requires patience, the ability to communicate clearly, and the ability to take action when everything feels like it is not working. Whenever you start an interview, you don't know…

- If and how the tech is going to screw up.
- What kind of problems you will have to work out with your guest.
- Whether or not your guest will be in a good mood for the interview.
- Whether you will be in a good mood to ask questions and be curious.
- … lots of other unanticipated variables.

Preparation for an interview is nothing like actually doing an interview. Because when you actually sit down with your guest and start recording, that's when all the unexpected stuff happens. This is both the thrill and the challenge of conducting interviews. If you can handle uncertainty like a champ, you will consistently record awesome interviews that you and your guests will be proud of.

There are some simple guidelines I have learned from conducting interviews with a range of personality types with a variety of different tech tools and for a range of different projects. The most important advice I can give you about actually conducting the interview is as follows:

Always conduct a check.

I use Zoom to record my podcast interviews. One of the benefits is that you can check things like audio and microphones.

Go through this process as a habit. One of the most important things that needs to be on your checklist is whether or not you have started the recording. Before you officially begin the interview, you need to manually check and make sure that you are RECORDING this interview which you put all your time and effort into arranging.

Spend fifteen minutes in any of the podcasting groups on Facebook. Read the horror stories of those who spent months working to get a top-quality guest, only to conduct an hour-long conversation and then discover that there is no audio of that interview. Always double-check to make sure you are recording. Make it part of your interview-conducting ritual.

Always read an introduction and start with a strong first question.

There are two great ways to ensure your interview gets off to a great start. The first is to read a well-written introduction that summarizes important biographical information and achievements of your guest. The second is to make sure you start with an effective first question.

The introduction you read when you start your podcast doesn't have to be the one that you use in the final edited version of the interview. (But it could be.)

The idea of reading an introduction is to help you transition from "setting up the interview" when your guest first arrives on Zoom (or whatever software you are using) to actually doing the interview. It also puts your guest at ease. It communicates that you know what you're doing and that you are serious about conducting a good interview and that you are familiar with who they are and what they do.

After introducing them and asking them how they are doing, launch confidently into a rapport-building question. This should be a friendly question. If you can, mention an achievement or something they are proud about. Basically, something that will put a smile on their face and let them pat themselves on the back. These kinds of questions can illicit boring answers, but you can cut them completely out when you edit the interview. Fret not. Your goal here is to get the guest talking and feeling comfortable.

One thing to not do is to hit them with tough or deep questions or make them feel uneasy or alarmed. Hold off on these. You need to build some connection with them and build a basic level of rapport before you ask them to share personal information that reflects their perspective in an engaging way.

Start with the small talk so that you can get to the big talk.

Pronounce the names in your introduction and questions correctly.

I should not have to tell you that you ought to read aloud both the introduction you prepared and the questions you brainstormed. Do you know how to correctly pronounce all names and words? You don't want to be wondering this while recording the podcast interview with your guest. Preparation is your friend. Read your introduction and questions aloud ahead of time.

Develop a sense for making the most of your "on-air" time.

I schedule my interviews for an hour. I plan on sticking to that hour whether we are on fire or not. I do go over the time often, but usually I ask for permission first.

When you schedule for an hour, that generally means you will get at least forty-five minutes of raw audio. It usually takes some time for the guest to arrive and get situated.

When you cut that raw footage down for an edited podcast, you might have anywhere from forty-five minutes to fifteen minutes. It depends on how aggressively you cut.

The point is keep an eye on the time. Make sure you cover the stuff you really want covered before you run out of time. Many of your guests will be busy, so plan on working with the time you scheduled.

Listen, Listen, Listen

There are two types of interviews that can happen once you start recording. The boring kind, where you stick only to your script of questions. And the fun kind, where you listen intently to your guest and take opportunities to ask follow-ups as time permits.

You don't have to think up highly complicated questions. Be simple. If you need inspiration, listen to interviewers like Terry Gross. Her brilliance as an interviewer isn't that she comes up with complicated questions. It's that she can angle into specific details by listening carefully and asking well-articulated follow-ups. It is all about the listening.

If you're starting out, you may feel unsafe with leaving the script. It's okay to feel that way for the first couple of interviews. As you grow in experience and confidence, let yourself go beyond the preparation you did before the interview.

When asking follow-ups, think about your interviewee's style.

In general, your guests are going to fall into one of two groups. They are going to be extremely intelligent and contextualize answers to your questions in very conceptually appealing ways. These people are intellectuals, and they are good at explaining their perspective in terms of ideas.

Another group of people contextualizes based on feelings and experiences. They will answer questions based on how events, relationships, or ideas have made them feel.

I've interviewed guests who fit both extremes. When asking follow-ups, it can be helpful to consider whether you have somebody who is intellectual or more emotional and then frame questions for these guests so that, as individuals, they may provide insightful answers.

When Following Up, Avoid Yes/No Questions

Want an example of how not to interview guests? Watch Chris Farley on *Saturday Night Live*. Lots of podcast episodes sound a bit too much like this exchange:

Paul McCartney: … It's great to be here.

Chris Farley: You remember when … you remember when you were with The Beatles?

Paul McCartney: Sure, sure.

Chris Farley: That was awesome!

Paul McCartney: Yeah, it was.

Chris Farley: Okay. Oh! You ... you remember when you went to Japan. And, uh, and at the airport, they arrested you 'cause you had some pot and it made all the papers and everything?

Paul McCartney: Well, to be honest, Chris, I'd kind of like to forget all of that.

Chris Farley: IDIOT! That's so stupid! What a dumb question!

Paul McCartney: No, no, no, Chris. I get asked that all the time in interviews. Maria Shriver asked the same question last week.

Chris Farley: Really? Did you know that she's married to Arnold Schwarzenegger?

Paul McCartney: Yeah. I've heard that.

Chris Farley: Did you see Terminator?

Paul McCartney: No. I missed that one.

Chris Farley: That was a pretty awesome flick. Okay. You remember when you were with The Beatles, and you were supposed to be dead and, uh, there was all these clues that, like, uh, you played some song backwards, and it'd say, like, "Paul is Dead" and, uh, everyone thought that you were dead? Or something? That was, um, a hoax, right?

Paul McCartney: Yeah. I wasn't really dead.

Chris Farley: Right. Umm. You remember Beatlemania?

The interview is intentionally awkward for comedic purposes. But one reason the answers are so superficial is because they are framed in a way to get a Yes/No answer.

When you do an interview and only ask Yes or No questions, you stay stuck in the interviewer's perspective. Chris Farley is not drawing out Paul McCartney's perspective. He is simply dragging McCartney through his own perspective with this endless cycle of polar questions.

Watch the SNL clip here for full effect:
https://www.nbc.com/saturday-night-live/video/the-chris-farley-show-paul-mccartney/2868143

Unfortunately, you will often hear real podcast hosts conducting interviews like the kind Chris Farley is doing as a comedian. Occasional yes/no framed questions are okay, but when your whole interview is structured this way, your interview is doomed to be boring. You will only get superficial answers.

Ask your guest open-ended questions that require interesting ideas and storytelling. Force the interviewee to construct answers that reflect their perspective—the experiences, insights, education, and ideas that made them worth inviting onto your show.

What if you are not getting good answers to your questions?

Do not blame the guest. (Even if they deserve it.) Your job is to be the person that brings out the perspective. Ask different questions until you get more meaningful responses. Focus on your end of the communication and let the chips fall where they may.

What if things don't go to plan because of tech issues?

Calmly work through the problem. Look for solutions. Make suggestions to your guest. Do not get frustrated or angry because this can make the guest uncomfortable.

It can make you feel desperate when things aren't working, but I have never had a guest complain about tech difficulties (and I've had some epic experiences in the tech issues department). Again, embrace uncertainty, even if it is in the form of tech issues.

As you are interviewing people who you want to connect with, consider this an opportunity to show people how you work under pressure. Communicate clearly, stay positive and enjoyable to work with, and use your problem-solving skills when technology goes awry.

Conducting interviews is scary. But they are also fun. It is only when you embrace the interview process that you will begin to recognize that things will not always go according to plan and that your best bet is to take things as they come and react as best as you're able.

Actions Steps:

- Have you scheduled interviews? What are you waiting for? Pitch guests so you can get them recorded.

- Test your equipment. In the previous chapter, I outlined a basic podcast setup that has a minimal cost. Take action; buy your tools and test them out.

- In addition to your tools, make sure you subscribe to a service such as Zoom, StreamYard, SquadCast, or Riverside so you can conduct your interviews.

- Live with other family members? Tell people when you are doing interviews. That way, they will keep their voices and activities down to "a mild roar" whilst you record.

CHAPTER ELEVEN:

Grow Your Confidence as an Interviewer

By now you have recorded or will record an interview. Congratulations!

Hopefully, you walk away with a solid recording. If you prepare and set the foundation for success, you will likely have a great experience. If not, that's okay. Because whether that recording was solid or not, you are going to become good at interviews by practicing them over and over. Interviews require you to build a set of important skills. Practicing interviews helps you to grow and develop.

You get good at something by learning about it, trying it out, refining your approach, and repeating the process. Plunge yourself into the process so that you can master the art of the interview and, in so doing, expand your sphere of influence in effective ways.

As you are doing interviews, there are some good guidelines that can help you grow in skill and confidence. Here are nine important guidelines to remember:

Eat well, sleep well, and drink enough water before the interview.

Come to every interview at the top of your game. Yes, there will be times when you do an interview while tired or hungry. But don't make this a habit.

Try to make sure that you are well-fed and well-hydrated before going into an interview. That extra edge of alertness makes a difference and will help you get better audio.

Also, make sure you use the bathroom before doing an interview. You want to stay both hydrated and relieved! There are many humorous stories of journalists who have had to balance the stress of a high-stakes interview alongside the call of nature. Make it a habit to visit the bathroom before your interviews start so that you do not have to interrupt the flow of the conversation.

Own your voice, accept your voice, consider ways for improvement.

Chances are good that you are not one hundred percent happy with your voice.

You may wish it sounded different. Tougher. Softer. Stronger. Gentler. Smoother. Sexier. And so on!

Right now, the best thing you can do is decide that you accept your voice. You accept your voice for what it sounds like, you are proud of that voice, and you want it to be the best it can be. With that in mind, you can look up vocal exercises or hire trainers to help you make the most of your voice. But before you can do anything, you need to own the voice—imperfections and all.

Consider mindfulness strategies.

Mindfulness can be one of the best ways to hone your craft as an interviewer. It can help make you more confident, thoughtful, and engaged.

There are a lot of approaches to "mindfulness."

One of my favorites is self-hypnosis. The best book I have read on the topic is Dr. Richard Nongard's *The Seven Most Effective Methods of Self-Hypnosis: How to Create Rapid Change in Your Health, Wealth, and Habits.* It is a quick read, and it will help you develop the confidence necessary for conducting interviews with world-class professionals.

Practice your interview prep sheet.

You know that interview prep sheet we talked about in Chapter 8? Practice it. Read it aloud. Let yourself find the words you can't pronounce, awkward sentence structures, or poorly formed question structures BEFORE you do the interview.

Plus, being confident that you are prepared will free up your mental focus on whether you are prepared or not. This will help you stay at the top of your game.

Practice effective conversation and interview techniques.

How often can you practice interview and conversation skills? Always. Take advantage of opportunities with friends, family, and work peers. Engage them in conversation. When they are telling a story, ask them follow-ups that help them express themselves with a great deal of depth. Every conversation is an opportunity to practice skills related to listening and asking follow-up questions.

Translate nervous energy into confidence.

Feel nervous before an interview? That is a good sign. That means you are taking the process seriously. Reframe "I feel nervous" into "I take this seriously and will do an awesome job." How we channel our emotions often determines whether they become our friend or our enemy. Use nerves before the interview to help you step into a proactive role of confidence.

Accept that all good interviews have hiccups.

You are going to be humming along, doing a great interview. Then you will have tech difficulties, or you are going to feel like a fool because you stumbled over your words, or you will feel awkward when a question you ask falls flat.

These things happen.

Good interviews you listen to are often (if not usually) edited to sound flawless and dramatic. You will also edit your podcast interviews. So, embrace the interview process with all its warts and realize that you can cut out the things that are not engaging later.

Learn how to be comfortable with silence.

A lot of newbie interviewers can't stand silence. Asking a question and then not having the guest answer immediately can be extremely uncomfortable.

An important point to know is that silence is an interviewer's friend.

While it can put some pressure on the interviewee, it means that he or she is really thinking about their answer. The answers you get after a long pause can be some of the most original and interesting answers given during the interview. So, keep quiet and let them consider the question. You can always edit out the long pauses and false starts.

Learn habits that help you speak without stumbling and stuttering.

Stuttering and stumbling over words can be a challenge. One way to beat this is to practice habits that help you avoid these behaviors. Example: Always feel anxious? This can be one of many factors that cause stumbling and stuttering. Practice habits that reduce your anxiety. Small changes can make big differences.

Listen to yourself on record.

Listen to your recordings. Do not fear them. Accept where you are at and identify small actionable things you can do to be a better interviewer. Things I've learned that I need to work on include…

- Speaking slower.
- Channeling enthusiasm more naturally.

- Rambling less, cutting to the chase.

Listen to your old recordings not to beat yourself up, but to identify ways in which you can turn your abilities from good to great. You are going to spend your entire life improving. Embrace this journey and take simple actionable steps that help you grow and improve.

Action Steps:

- Go through the list of suggestions in this chapter. Pick one that you think will help you the most. What is one thing you can do today that will help you apply this idea in your life or interviews so that you can grow in your confidence and skills? Take action.

- Schedule interviews. Ideally, you want to launch your podcast with three complete episodes, and you want to have a couple of episodes scheduled in advance.

CHAPTER TWELVE:

Post-interview Steps You Must Take

Many podcasting guides talk about the post-interview stage strictly in terms of what you need to do to get your podcast interview edited and published. However, this book is about how to grow your sphere of influence through your podcast. Therefore, it is not only necessary to cover the basics of how to get your podcast episode published but also the details of how to cultivate your network by taking the right steps once an interview is concluded.

Phase 1: The Networking Side, Post-Interview

The basic rules of networking with guests AFTER the interview is as follows:

- Save their contact information.
- Send an email thanking them for engagement.
- Consider connecting with them on social media.
- Make sure your socials reflect your personal brand.

Hopefully, it is apparent that when you use this strategy for networking purposes, the idea is that you are building connections in your niche before you need them. That way, if areas for mutual cooperation emerge later, you will already have a connection where value was exchanged.

Do not be a networking jerk.

In his book *Never Eat Alone*, Keith Ferrazzi warns professionals to avoid being "the networking jerk," and he provides several best practices. For me, there are five important takeaways from his book that can help podcasters become networking superstars instead of networking jerks.

- *Don't be superficial.* "Have something to say and say it with passion. Make sure you have something to offer when you speak and offer it with sincerity... networking is not a secret society with some encoded handshake practiced for its own virtue. We must bring virtue to it."

- *Think in terms of providing value.* "In connecting online and off, you're only as good as what you give away… providing information, creative content, links, or even just empathy to a community of like-minded individuals... [these] are the stars of today's digital world..."

- *Treat people with dignity.* "You must treat people with respect up and down the ladder." This concept that all people possess inherent dignity should not be a platitude; it should be an actual worldview that is expressed through your actions and how you treat others. When people accept the humanity of people first and want us to have empowered "social roles," we bond with those people instantly.

- *Be yourself and allow yourself to be vulnerable, enthusiastic, and open.* "Coy games may work in a bar, but not when you're looking to establish a deeper, more meaningful connection."

- *Be personal.* "Nothing comes off as less sincere than receiving a mass email addressed to a long list of recipients." An example relevant to podcasting: Do not follow up an interview with a generic "Thank you for being one of our guests…" sort of message. Address it specifically to them, mention what you had fun discussing, and remind them that you appreciate the time they took to talk.

Remember to think in terms of value exchange as your network grows bigger and bigger. It's not about how special you are; it's about what you are doing to serve other people in your niche—whether that is your audience and mentees, your peers, or your mentors and leaders. Adopt an attitude of service.

By developing and hosting your podcast, you are creating a space for amazing conversations. There is both personal and professional value in inviting somebody into such a space to share their perspective. Provide value through this connection, and you will potentially set the stage for value exchange in the future if there are opportunities for mutual benefit.

Cultivate an authentic understanding of your personal brand and interact in a way that is consistent with it.

A priority of this book is building your sphere of influence through your podcast efforts. That means interacting with people effectively. And the basis upon which you interact with people is rooted in your personal brand identity.

Some of you may have a very good idea about personal branding.

Others might still be hammering out important aspects of your personal brand.

Regardless, one of the best books on this topic is Catherine Kaputa's *You Are a Brand!* which I first encountered as an assigned reading as a graduate student in the field of communication at Southern New Hampshire University. It offers an intuitive approach to thinking about your personal brand. And don't worry, though it served as a textbook in an accredited college class, the book is quite readable and enjoyable. It provides actionable and practical steps you can start applying right away.

Whether you are a newbie in your niche or you have experience, think about cultivating your personal brand in a way that is consistent with your goals and the value you want to provide to your niche.

Politics, politics.

One final consideration. You may have noticed that much of what I discuss involves you opening up your social media profiles and connecting with individuals in your niche. Think of your social media accounts as fair game for everybody who will enjoy your podcast—guests and audience members alike.

Accordingly, consider to what extent you ought to be expressing your viewpoints about politics.

Make no mistake about it. Partisan political posts turn people off.

Chances are good that you will lose credibility and likability if you insist on shoving your biased political viewpoints down the throats of other biased people. For those here in the United States, this is not the 1990s with relatively boring candidates such as Bill Clinton and Bob Dole. Political discourse has increasingly become more outrageous. People on all sides have less tolerance and feel more threatened.

I make extra efforts to not get too political. Nothing political AND negative, in particular. Snarky political posts cost you credibility, and if you are trying to build your sphere of influence, it might be time to take the high road and not post such content.

There are exceptions. For example, if you are a political activist, it might be okay if your profile is totally filled with partisan memes. But err on the side of caution if your niche is apolitical.

People are burned out with strict win-lose conflicts and judgmental attitudes, such as those reflected in the game of politics. They are increasingly seeking empathy and respect and are attracted to connections that promise to help fulfill these basic human needs.

Nobody is perfect. But operate *mostly* from a perspective of kindness, truth, and goodwill for people you agree with as well as those you do not. In so doing, you will create a magnetic brand presence. Indirectly, this will serve you well in your podcasting journey.

Hopefully, these tips will help you approach the networking side of your podcast with a greater degree of clarity. Next, let's discuss getting your podcast produced.

Phase 2: The Production Side, Post-Interview

Our goal on the production side of podcasting is to sound professional. Good content combined with professional delivery will maximize engagement and will help ensure that your guest is willing to share the interviews you do with their own audience.

At its most basic level, this process involves three steps:

- Edit the episode.
- Upload it to a podcast hosting service.
- Write show notes.

Who will edit your podcast?

If you read Chapter 6, you have a good idea about what pieces you need to edit together to create a compelling podcast episode. The question is, how do you do it?

Your options are to:

- Do it yourself.
- Pay somebody else to do it.

Personally, I edit my own podcasts. That said, there are pros and cons to both options, and which you choose will depend on what resources you can best leverage. Some of you will have more time, and others will have more money and thus can outsource.

When you hire an editor, the obvious benefits are that you save time, and you do not need to learn how to use software such as Audacity (which is what I use to edit my podcast episodes) or Adobe Audition. Disadvantages are that you are not able to implement your own personal vision as deeply into the process and that regular editing for weekly or biweekly podcasts can be expensive for those who are not making a lot of money with their show.

Do you have more time? If so, get started with a program like Audacity and edit your own episodes. If you are not savvy with technology and are willing to spend a bit of money, hire a professional on a site like Fiverr or Upwork to do it for you.

Pick a host for your podcast.

You want to get your podcast published in the major podcast directories. This includes Apple Podcasts, Google Podcasts, Spotify, Audible, and Stitcher. How do you achieve this? You subscribe to an online podcast hosting company such as Buzzsprout.

Of all the podcast hosting companies, Buzzsprout is the one I have worked with in the past, and it is one that I have had amazing experiences with.

Basically, you upload your new episodes and schedule them for publication. You are allotted a certain number of hours every month (based on what plan you select), and when your podcast is published, it will automatically appear in all the directories that you have submitted for listing.

Why use a podcast hosting company like Buzzsprout? Because it makes the delivery of your podcasts easy to manage. Simply hitting the "Publish" button and then having your episode go into all the major podcast directories like Spotify and Apple Podcasts makes your life easier. It's also dirt cheap. I pay around $18 a month to host *Jazz and Blues Affinity*.

Buzzsprout is user-friendly, and they keep their training materials up to date. It is super easy to get started, and that's why I recommend it for new podcasters.

Write your show notes.

Look at podcasts you enjoy. How do they structure their show notes? In general, you should include:

- A biographical sketch of the person you are interviewing.
- A summary of what you are going to discuss in the podcast episode.
- Links to anything the guest wants to promote.

You can also include calls to action that help draw people into your sphere of influence. That means asking them to connect with you online, check out your book, sign up for your email list, and so on.

And there you have it! This is a guide to the basics of post-interview steps that should be taken to help ensure that you create winning connections with as many of your guests as possible so that you create an extremely engaging podcast episode that listeners love.

Action Steps:

- Decide if you are going to hire an editor to create your podcast episodes or if you are going to edit them yourself.
- Select a podcast hosting company such as Buzzsprout to help you list your podcast in the major directories as well as upload new episodes.
- As you conduct interviews, use the best practices described in this chapter to forge basic quality connections and thereby grow your sphere of influence.

CHAPTER THIRTEEN:

90-Day Roadmap for Launching Your Interview Podcast

It took me about ninety days to launch *Jazz and Blues Affinity*. I gave myself that amount of time to figure things out, and I proceeded to do just that—I read countless books, considered my previous experience with library projects and *Show Me Rolla*, and began studying various podcasts.

Within ninety days, I had a podcast.

I made some screwups. I spent a lot of time confused. And the ideas you have been reading about in this book are designed to help you skip over some of the learning curves you encounter when you decide to start a podcast specifically for networking purposes.

This is a basic roadmap. There are a few additional steps spelled out here, but more or less, it simply reiterates the action steps given to you at the end of Chapters 4 to 12. Make sure you go and read those chapters. They provide more context about how to do these steps.

This simple roadmap would have helped me, and hopefully, it helps you. Follow these steps, and you will have an interview podcast with three published episodes and two scheduled episodes. You can do this!

Month 1:

- Mindsets are the foundation for everything. So write down the following: *I am a podcast host who talks to people in [your niche] because I am passionate about better understanding the people and perspectives behind [your niche].* Creating a podcast where you explore perspectives is an easy and effective way to begin building connections with people in your niche.

- Cultivate an attitude of curiosity. Start studying good interviews in the world of podcasting as well as in more traditional forms of media such as television and radio. Become a student of conversation. Consider interviewing an asset to your personal brand and consistently work on improving.

- Start practicing clearer speech and conversations in everyday life. Focus on being more present and engaged in all your social interactions, and podcast conversations will become easier.

- Brainstorm possible target audiences. Then narrow it down to one group.

- Research your target listeners.
- Create an avatar that represents your target audience.
- Create an elevator pitch that briefly and engagingly tells your avatar exactly what your podcast is about—and why it matters.
- Create a name for your podcast.
- List out forty or fifty possible interview guests that you would like to invite.

Month 2:

- Have a professional intro and outro recorded for your podcast. You can outsource this at www.voices.com or www.fiverr.com. This is what you will use to help brand the show, and it helps give your program a more professional feel.
- Evaluate what technology you need and what you already have. Remember, to start recording interviews virtually, you need a desktop computer, an internet connection, virtual recording software, a web camera, a microphone (and a pop filter), and a pair of headphones. Check out my website for a list of links that will allow you to duplicate my inexpensive but effective setup. https://professionalpodcastcreation.com/podcastequipmentforbeginners/
- Use the BEST test to evaluate your list of potential interviewees. If you are just starting out with podcasting,

consider individuals you already have a connection to, as they can be easier to pitch.

- Pick five or six of the names you brainstormed. Craft a short message asking them to be on your show. Look up their contact info and send them an email or direct message. Get the ball rolling! Pick five or six names from your list every week, and chances are good you will have plenty of podcast guests for your show.

- Decide what you are going to use to record your interviews. I use Zoom. Other popular options include StreamYard, SquadCast, and Riverside.

- Test your podcasting equipment as well as the software you are going to use to record your interview.

- Select your podcast hosting company. I recommend www.buzzsprout.com.

Month 3:

- Hopefully, by now, you have as many as three—and potentially as many as six or seven—"Yes" responses to interview requests. (If not, send more requests, and don't forget to ask people you already know.) Make sure you follow up and get your interviews scheduled.

- Prepare for these interviews by creating preparation sheets that include a brief introduction and a list of fifteen to eighteen questions.

- Record your interviews. Save the raw audio somewhere safe. Back it up in at least one other spot, such as in Dropbox.

- Set a launch date. You can promote this heavily if you have a big audience, or you can simply do a soft launch by just picking a day and dropping your first episodes when that day arrives. Ideally, you will start by publishing three episodes and scheduling two.

- Edit your episodes yourself or hire a professional to edit them for you.

- Upload your initial batch of episodes to major podcast directories such as Spotify, Apple Podcasts, or Stitcher via your podcast hosting company. Ideally, you want to launch your podcast with three complete episodes, and you want to have a couple of episodes scheduled in advance.

- As you finish conducting interviews, use the best practices described in this chapter to forge basic quality connections and thereby grow your sphere of influence.

CHAPTER FOURTEEN:

It's Time to Grow Your Sphere of Influence

When you first picked up this book, you wondered if podcasting could be a viable strategy to help you build a bigger and better presence in your niche. Regardless of whether you're a beginning professional or an experienced one, you can rapidly grow your sphere of influence at any stage of your career by launching a podcast that fosters authentic conversations with significant people in your niche.

Keith Ferrazzi wrote in his book *Never Eat Alone*, "We are the very product of the people and networks to which we are connected. Who you know determines who you are—how you feel, how you act, and what you achieve."

Initiating relationships is a key step to expanding your own network and thereby increasing your potential. What better way to initiate contacts than to start a podcast where you have permission to invite world-class professionals for one-on-one conversations. As you interview the significant people in your niche, you will feel more confident. As you make connections and create conversations, you will feel the empowering energy that comes from proactively engaging the community of your niche in relevant ways.

Just a week before writing this final chapter, the library for which I did the *Missouri Bicentennial Series* received a letter with "ATTN: Derek Zboran" marked at the bottom left-hand corner. My supervisor tossed me the envelope.

"You got mail, Derek."

"For me? What is it?" I asked.

"I dunno," my supervisor replied, adding: "Could be anthrax." (Librarian assistants have a morbid sense of humor. It is our coping mechanism.) After a brief consideration of this possibility, I grabbed a pair of scissors and slit open the envelope.

Inside was a single piece of paper. It read: "Dear Derek... I have had the good fortune to discover your interviews on the Rolla Public Library website, which you have posted on YouTube. The discussions that you have had with authors, particularly with the author of the biography of Dale Carnegie, are really well done. You have clearly done your homework, and you do a fine job of allowing the authors to tell their stories. Libraries are a community treasure, and your educational outreach has enriched Rolla and anyone else who has had the good fortune to watch your interviews. Well done!"

These words made me soar as I realized that the *Missouri Bicentennial Series* had achieved exactly what I sought to accomplish. Thanks to basic digital technology, I reached out to a range of world-class professionals in my niche (in this case, Missouri history), conducted good interviews with several of them, and created connections. In so doing, not only did I increase the value of my personal brand but also that of the library in which I work.

My hope is that you take the tools from this book to create an interview podcast of value in your own niche that elevates your personal brand while also making a difference in a community you love.

Your journey to being a successful podcast host is not about fame, or trying to fake a superficial personality, or trying to maximize how much you can profit from your show. It is a journey in which you create, foster, and build a space in which the people of your niche feel welcomed, appreciated, and engaged through conversation. It starts when you identify as an interviewer and embrace this as a significant skill for professionals of the twenty-first century. It takes on a life of its own when you define what that space looks like and establish a structure for delivering interview content in a professional episodic format. It gains momentum as you begin reaching out to potential guests, preparing interviews for those who agree, and then conducting and recording those interviews. And it begins to make a difference (for your brand and in your niche) when you publish an episode that makes your guest feel proud to have been on your show and which engages your growing base of listeners.

The best way to begin growing your sphere of influence through podcasting is to start taking action today. What can you apply from this book right now that will help you build a successful interview podcast? Acknowledge that you are stepping into the role of the interviewer and that you are the right person to conduct engaging conversations with top individuals in your niche. Then build the foundation of your podcast by determining what kind of space you are going to create and what type of avatar you are going to serve. Once you have your foundation, you need to buckle your seat belt and get ready for the wild phase of requesting interviews, getting "Yes" responses, and then doing the work to see that the interview is prepared, scheduled, and conducted successfully. Do not strive for perfection. Everything starts with a first step. Taking that first step is the perfect action for you to take right now as you finish this book.

Whether you are eighteen or eighty-eight, you are a growing professional. You have value to provide in your niche. And you desire to grow a sphere of influence that helps you share your value with others while becoming more connected in the field that you enjoy serving as a professional. You already have what it takes to conduct quality conversations with top professionals in your niche. Now is the time to get the ball rolling. Get your podcast launched and start conducting powerful conversations.

I assist professionals grow their sphere of influence by helping them start successful interview podcasts. If you have a podcast idea and want me to help you with it, visit my website: https://www.professionalpodcastcreation.com/
You can also contact me at professionalpodcastcreation.com.

By checking out my website and signing up for my email list, you will also get free access to helpful resources that will help you successfully navigate the journey to a successful interview podcast. Thanks for reading this book, and best wishes on your career and podcasting pursuits!

Acknowledgements

The book you're reading is the product of two years of experiments with podcasting. Between 2020 and 2022, I have spent much of my life conceptualizing, planning, and recording interviews and podcasts. I've tried stuff that succeeded and stuff that failed.

There are several important people who contributed to my successes in podcasts. More importantly, they have helped cultivate within me the ability for achieving future successes.

First, I want to thank my parents, Jim and Shirley Zboran.

Jim was the one who first suggested I try out podcasting—he was the one who first planted the seed. Many of my greatest adventures start with Jim in one way or another. As for Shirley, she is my first and foremost fan, listening to and sharing every episode I record on her social media profiles. It's fun to know that there is one person who will be enjoying my interviews no matter what.

I also want to give a special shoutout to my grandmothers. Rita Zboran is a special person who encouraged me to pursue my master's degree in a topic I was passionate about. She has supported me wholeheartedly in the pursuit of a communications degree specializing in new media and marketing. Pursuing this degree has exposed me to a well-rounded body of evidence, ideas, and trends in communication which has both directly and indirectly supported my efforts in podcasting. Marjorie Holt is also a special person who has consistently encouraged me in my interview projects. It is always fun to talk with somebody who encourages, and Marjorie does just that in each of our phone calls.

A big thanks to Library Director Rebecca Buckley and former Library Board President Diana Ahmad for helping me at the library. Rebecca has been part mentor, part boss, and part cheerleader; I appreciate her. Diana has also been supportive and willing to lend her participation in my podcasting projects. My work in library services will always be a significant part of how I approach the development of media projects, and Rebecca and Diana are two people who were pivotal in shaping how I experienced library work over the last couple of years during the unusual challenges created by the COVID pandemic.

In terms of getting this book written and learning how to think like a "creative," I want to thank Richard Nongard, creator of the www.TwelveWeekBook.com program. He has built an awesome and supportive community of writers. I always look forward to building my creative habit in Richard's writing classes.

Finally, I want to give a special thank you to my editor, Ita de Groot. She was gracious with this newbie book author and took me through all the steps in a way that minimized my hassle and struggle. She also was committed to doing a great job during the editing process. Furthermore, her feedback on my writing, particularly that my natural writing voice is friendly and helpful, has provided me with great insights about how to continue developing my natural voice as a writer.

Made in the USA
Monee, IL
08 November 2026

67971458R00090